Fishing and Managing the Trent in the Medieval Period (7th–14th Century)

Excavations at Hemington Quarry (1998–2000), Castle Donington, UK

Lynden P. Cooper
Susan Ripper

with contributions by
Matt Beamish, Jennifer Browning, Nicholas J. Cooper,
Robert Howard, Patrick Marsden, Angela Monckton,
Anita Radini and Deborah Sawday

BAR British Series 633

2017

Published in 2017 by
BAR Publishing, Oxford

BAR British Series 633

Fishing and Managing the Trent in the Medieval Period (7th–14th Century)

ISBN 978 1 4073 1617 8

COVER IMAGE *Eel basket associated with weir HL12.*

Printed in England

BAR
PUBLISHING

BAR titles are available from:

BAR Publishing
122 Banbury Rd, Oxford, OX2 7BP, UK
EMAIL info@barpublishing.com
PHONE +44 (0)1865 310431
FAX +44 (0)1865 316916
www.barpublishing.com

Dedication

Patrick Clay has been instrumental in developing the alluvial archaeology agenda of the Middle Trent from the 1980s to the present, a time of great flux in British Archaeology. He directed the early work at Pontylue (Hemington) Quarry, forming a long-term collaboration with the independent archaeologist Chris Salisbury. Since the growing commercialisation of archaeology in the 1990s he has managed the Hemington Bridges project and the work that is featured in this volume. We thank him for his constant and amiable support.

Acknowledgements

ULAS would like to thank Lafarge Aggregates Ltd. for allowing access to the site and for funding the archaeological work. Owen Bathom and Ian Smith, the on-site representatives of Lafarge Aggregates, are thanked for their help in co-ordinating the works within the extraction programme. Thanks are also due to Anne Graf, then Senior Planning Archaeologist, Leicestershire County Council. Simon Collcutt, Geoarchaeologist, Oxford Archaeological Associates.

Anita Radini would like to express her gratitude to Allan Hall for the help and support with the identification and analysis of the waterlogged wood assemblage.

The report is compiled from information recorded on site by the authors and ULAS staff Matt Beamish, Jen Browning, Jon Coward, Simon Chapman, Sophie Clarke, Michael Derrick, Tony Gnanaratnam, James Gossip, Rufus Henderson, Tim Higgins, Wayne Jarvis, Keith Johnson, James Meek, Vicki Score, Martin Shore, Jo Sturgess and John Thomas. Thanks to ULAS specialist collaborators Matthew Beamish, Jennifer Browning, Nick Cooper, Patrick Marsden, Angela Monckton Anita Radini and Deborah Sawday. Thanks to Patrick Clay for managing the project.

Thanks are also due to Richard Darrah (Ancient Timber Specialist), Graham Morgan (conservator), Dr. A. Brandon (British Geological Survey), Robert Howard and Ian Tyres (tree ring analysis).

Volunteers: Caroline Mills, Shirley Bowley, David Budge, Alan Cormack, Sue Hadcock, Sue Ebbins, David Hancock, Norman Lewis, Brian Miller, Alan Palfreyman and Keith Reedman.

Illustrations: Photographs were taken by the field excavation team and Chris Salisbury, post-excavation illustrations were compiled by Susan Ripper with the help of Steve Baker. Hari Jacklin drew the millstone roughouts.

The authors would also like to thank Peter Carter, Maggie Cooper and Cesca Beamish for their very useful observations and generous comments on the arts of basket making, wicker work and eel catching. Matt Beamish provided invaluable help and sound advice on timber technology and alluvial archaeology, all with good humour. The late Chris Salisbury was a good companion and provided a wealth of knowledge on rivers and fisheries.

UNIVERSITY OF
LEICESTER
Archaeological Services

Contents

List of Figures

List of Tables

Abstract

Palaeochannels of the river Trent revealed at Hemington Quarry have provided a geoarchaeological record from the Late Glacial to medieval period. The later palaeochannels have provided a rich archaeological vein with numerous riverine and riparian structures dating from the late 7th to 14th centuries. These have included mills, bridges, fish weirs and other installations. This volume describes the alluvial archaeology revealed in a long-term watching brief at Hemington Quarry Western Extension from 1998–2000 as well as riverine structures from Hemington Quarry Eastern Extension Phase 5 excavated in 1998. As with the remains of the medieval Hemington Bridges (Ripper and Cooper 2009) all of the structures described in this report were preserved due to the dynamism of the Trent, being rapidly buried under advancing sand and gravel bars and/or flood deposits.

The structural remains offer a rare glimpse of a developing inland fishery with particular evidence for the passive fishing of yellow and silver eels. These are not separate species but physiological stages in the life cycle of eels: The young eels that enter the waterways of the British Isles are elvers and these swim upstream where they quickly mature as yellow eels. These live in rivers and other bodies of inland water for several years. Yellow eels develop into sexually mature silver eels and these migrate downstream to the sea in the autumn, eventually reaching the spawning grounds of the Sargasso Sea. This predictable autumnal migration would have provided a valuable resource for the medieval fisheries, encouraging the installation of semi-permanent fish weirs to allow catching of eels *en masse*.

The earliest structures were a series of well-preserved early medieval (Anglo-Saxon) fish traps comprising lines of posts that supported wattle fences, these 'leaders' arranged to divert fish into nets or baskets. These structures can be termed fish weirs or hedge weirs (after the Anglo-Saxon *haecwera*). The V-shaped planforms of two fish weirs, each with their apex or 'eye' located downstream, indicate that they were specialised structures to catch silver eels as they migrated back to the sea in the autumn. Another arrangement of posts converged to a closed, upstream V shape. This effectively created an area with restricted channel flow, where the smaller yellow eels were caught in small basket traps and eel tufts, tied bundles of brushwood containing bait. This area became a repository for much organic material culture. The basketry, wattle panels and wooden artefacts were well-preserved and provide rare evidence for artisanship of the period.

Immediately adjacent to the medieval channel were two early medieval (Anglo-Saxon) structures evident from sub-square arrangements of post-holes. These may be smoke-houses or bothies related to the riparian and riverine exploitation.

Documentary and cartographic research identifies the later medieval sites as parts of the manorial river fishery of Castle Donington. A large stone and timber weir, a likely mill dam, of the 12th century was utilised as a fishing station evident from two massive eel baskets. One basket was anchored on top of the weir whilst the other lay at the mouth of a V-shaped wooden structure built to funnel water at the far end of the weir. This basket was exceptionally well preserved and comprised a 2m long cone-shaped willow trap. Large oak baseplates, with an abundance of disused joints, were used to prevent scouring at the mouth of the funnel of the weir. It is likely that they originated in a nearby riverine structure, probably from a disused water mill.

By the 14th century the manorial fishery is described as the net fishery. Several bank-side structures of early 14th century date are probably purpose-built net fishing stations. These stone-filled timber cribs were jetties that projected into the river and may have served to initiate scour pools and provide eddies that were attractive to salmonids. The jetties reflect the demise of weir fishing that had been banned by local and national legislation.

Introduction

Location and Setting

Hemington Quarry is located towards the centre of a wide floodplain (SK 459 302), up to 8km across, within the confluence zone of the rivers Trent, Derwent and Soar, with the Tame and the Dove not far upstream (Figure 1). The wide floodplain in this confluence zone is characterised by deep deposits of sand and gravel, the lower units deposited in the Devensian (Holme Pierrepont terrace) with an upper unit derived from reworking and deposition within the meander belts of the Holocene river system. The latter has been termed the Hemington Terrace but there are doubts about the validity of this term (John Carney, BGS, pers. comm.). Flanking the floodplain are deposits of the Holme Pierrepont Terrace. The floodplain gravels overlie a solid geology of formations of the Mercia Mudstone Group, comprising clay, mudstone and sandstone.

The confluence zone is characterised by considerable past channel migrations evident from the complex systems of intercutting palaeochannels visible on aerial photographs. This historical mobility is demonstrated by the sinuous nature of many of the parish and enclosure boundaries. These follow earlier courses of the river, well exemplified within the quarry site itself, where the pre-1974 county boundary partly follows the line of the modern Trent and partly a silted-up course (the 'Old Trent'), which, until 1994, formed the eastern limit of the quarry. Brown (2009) has presented a model of channel evolution in the Hemington Reach. For the period under discussion in this report (late 7th–14th century) there is a progression from a wandering braided gravel-bed river in the 8th–9th centuries, during the medieval warm period, to a braided river with flood-driven progressive flow switching in the 10th–12th centuries, in a period of Late Medieval climatic

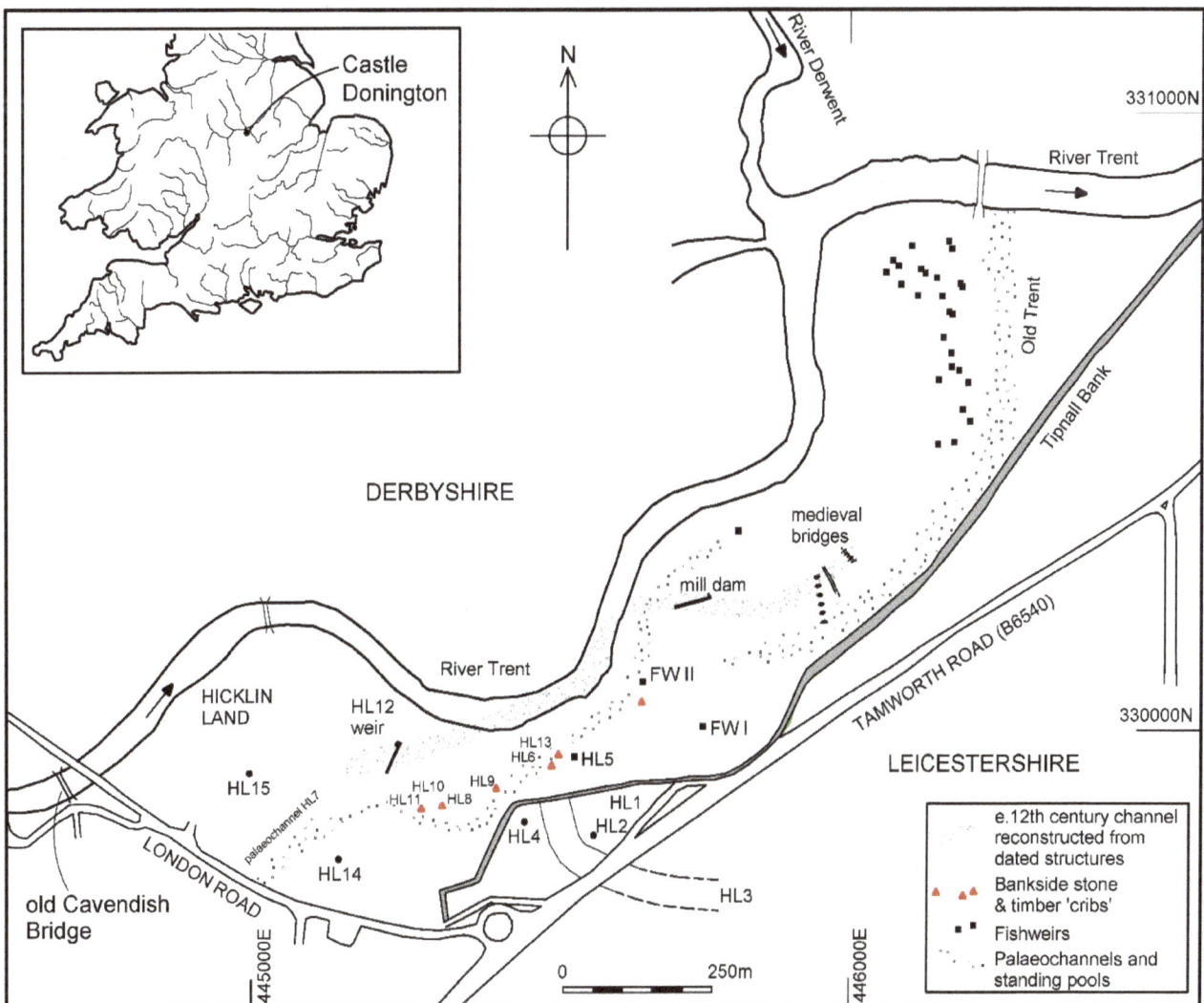

Figure 1: Location of the riverine structures located within Hemington Quarry.

deterioration, to an anastomosing channel in the 12th–17th centuries (Brown 2009, 158).

The quarry straddles the parish boundaries of Castle Donington and Lockington-Hemington in north-west Leicestershire, immediately south of the Trent and Derwent confluence. Prior to the 1974 boundary changes the north-western part of the quarry would have been in Shardlow and Great Wilne parish. The original 1985–94 quarry limits were defined by the modern Trent to the north and west, and the Old Trent to the east. The western extension (the subject of this report) was a meander belt of the Trent from around the 7th to 14th centuries, with the Old Trent representing the most easterly channel of the migrating river. The bridges and other riverine structures (Ripper and Cooper 2009) were all located within this meander belt, their exceptional survival due to their deep burial under sand and gravel deposited by the river.

This report describes the results of archaeological fieldwork undertaken between autumn 1998 and summer of 2000 at the Hemington Quarry western extension (Figure 2), work originally commissioned by Lafarge-Redlands Ltd., the fore-runner of Lafarge Aggregates Ltd.. A medieval palaeochannel system preserved structures and artefacts that can be related to the Castle Donington manorial fishery and water mill. Three comparable sites recorded in the Quarry's eastern extension (Phase 5) recorded earlier in 1998 are also included. These parts of the quarry mostly lay within the parish of Castle Donington, Leicestershire (NGR SK 45 29, Figure 1). Archaeological works were required

under Condition No. 35 of the planning permission granted for mineral extraction at Hemington Quarry Western Extension (termed 'Hicklin Land' in Planning Application 96/0714/7). A desk-based assessment (Cooper *et al.* 1996) outlined the strong likelihood of significant archaeological structures, sediments and artefacts based upon the previous discovery of palaeochannels, the Hemington bridges, a mill dam and some forty-one fish weir structures (Ripper and Cooper 2009). A geomorphological report (Brown 1997) provided a model for the evolution of the channel system in the proposed quarry area (see also Brown 2009 for the wider Hemington Reach). Collcutt's (1998) geomorphological assessment of the area around Hemington Quarry complemented Brown's work and provided a wider model of channel evolution in the Hemington Reach of the middle Trent.

Archaeological fieldwork at Hemington Quarry started in 1985 with the discovery of a vertical-wheeled water mill of 12th century date (Clay and Salisbury 1990). Thereafter a regular watching brief was maintained at the quarry recording 43 examples of post alignments, some with attached wattle panels (Salisbury 1990; 1991b; 1993; 1994). Most, if not all, of these structures are examples of fish weirs similar to those recorded upstream at Colwick, Nottinghamshire (Losco-Bradley and Salisbury 1979; Salisbury 1981). In 1993 Salisbury made his most spectacular discovery with the Hemington bridges, three successive structures that were subject to full excavation by Leicestershire Archaeological Unit (LAU). The Hemington Bridges project was the subject of a University of Leicester

Figure 2: Google Earth *c.* 1999. Aerial view of Hicklin Land showing the area illustrated in Figure 1.

monograph (Ripper and Cooper 2009), supported by an English Heritage publication grant.

Subsequent extensions to the quarry were subject to improved archaeological provisions by way of Planning Policy Guidance note 16 [3] allowing for funded monitoring of extraction works with contingent funds for further excavation should significant remains be revealed. Since 1998 extraction moved back into the rich archaeological vein of the medieval channel system revealing three fish weir complexes, six jetty structures and a large stone weir, thought to be a basket weir fishery re-using a former water mill dam.

The fish weirs reported herein, and the vast majority of the excavated fish weirs from the Middle Trent, were constructed as two lines of converging posts, or 'leaders', having a downstream apex or 'eye'. The gap at the apex would have been fished with a net or basket trap. Such structures were almost certainly built to catch silver eels on their downstream migration in the autumn (Losco-Bradley and Salisbury 1979; Salisbury 1981). The structures are identical to weirs used for catching silver eels on the River Bann (Mitchell 1965) which had downstream eyes indicating that they were purpose-built structures for catching silver eels (Salisbury 1981). After some years the yellow or brown eels, as they are variously described, undergo metamorphosis into silver eels, sexually mature eels ready for their return migration to the Sargasso Sea (Moriarty 1978). The fish undergo physiological changes, their fat content increasing, their guts shrink and their anal passage becomes fused. It is thought that low temperature may be a strong factor in the timing of this metamorphosis (Vøllestadt *et al.* 1986; Tesch 1977).

Methods

Deep alluvial cover prevented conventional archaeological trench evaluation so a mitigation strategy of staged work was proposed to deal with the likely threat to any surviving archaeological remains. The strategy was outlined in the Scheme of Archaeological Works (Collcutt 1997). A Design Specification for Archaeological Work (Clay 1997) detailed how this work was to be accomplished.

The agreed archaeological mitigation to the sand and gravel extraction was multi-staged. In 1998 a series of trial trenches were excavated on the Holme-Pierrepont terrace remnant. The Tipnall Bank earthwork was sectioned but dating evidence was not conclusive (an early Anglo-Saxon feature was sealed by the bank). Otherwise the results were negative. Thereafter there was a watching brief on aggregate extraction with contingent arrangements for funded excavations.

The watching brief was undertaken for ULAS by Lynden Cooper from 1998. This entailed a weekly site visit where the extraction faces were inspected for geoarchaeological deposits and structures. Periodically, where and when practical, the exposed faces were surveyed with a Total Station. Chris Salisbury also maintained his independent watching brief continuing his work from the mid-1980s, but there was considerable overlap and communication.

Contingent funds were agreed on a site by site basis with input from project manager Patrick Clay and Lynden Cooper (ULAS), and the consultant for LaFarge-Redlands, Simon Collcutt (Oxford Archaeological Associates). Every effort was made not to hinder extraction though occasionally extraction work had to be moved temporarily. The excavations were directed by Lynden Cooper and Susan Ripper. An assessment of the fieldwork results and a project design for post-excavation analysis and research were produced by Ripper and Cooper (2002).

Excavation Results: Structural Synopsis

Since archaeological work commenced in 1998 each archaeological site was assigned a group number, prefixed with HL (after 'Hicklin Land', the planning application title for this parcel of land). HL2 was a limited observation of a palaeosol and is not reported here. For the purposes of this report the structures have been grouped according to type and will be described under group headings. Three structures observed during Phase 5 of the Hemington Quarry Eastern Extension have also been included as their previous reporting was minimal (Fish weirs I and II and a stone and timber revetment or crib structure). Also included as an appendix is a short report on an assemblage of medieval mill paddles from several phases of quarry extraction.

- Fish weirs (HL5 and Fish weirs I and II)
- Settlement (HL4)
- Stone and timber jetties (HL6, 8, 10, 11, &13)
- Stone weir (HL12)
- Palaeochannels (HL1, 3, 7, 14 & 15)

Fish Weirs

Salisbury (1990, 1991a, b, 1993; Salisbury and Brown 2009) has reported many examples of fish weirs from Hemington Quarry with radiocarbon dates ranged from 8th – 12th centuries AD. Well-preserved examples of these 'hedge weirs' (OE *haecwera*, after Seebohm 1894) were also found downstream of the Trent at Colwick, Nottinghamshire (Losco-Bradley and Salisbury 1979 and 1988; Salisbury 1981) and show that their typical form was of two lines of piled posts, V-shaped in plan with an open, downstream apex. It is assumed that baskets or fyke nets were employed at the apex though, as yet, no archaeological evidence has been found. The structures were purpose built for the catching of silver eels on their downstream migration in the autumn (Losco-Bradley and Salisbury 1979; Salisbury 1981).

Three hedge weir type fishing stations are reported below in chronological order, starting with Fish weir II. The term 'fish weir' is retained as this is how they have been reported previously (Salisbury 1990, 1991a, b, 1993; Salisbury and Brown 2009; Cooper 2003). These stations comprised Fish weir I and Fish weir II from the Hemington Quarry Eastern

Extension Phase 5 (Cooper 1999, 91–97) and HL5 from the Western Extension (Figure 1). The latter is a complex of several post alignments including a conventional V-shaped structure plus ancillary lines. In addition there is a downstream complex of posts and wattle panels that was probably another type of passive fish trap, situated in the backwater behind one of the leaders of the main fish weir. This has been termed an 'eel weir' as there was good evidence for the trapping of yellow eels.

Fish Weir II (Late 7th–8th Century AD)

Fish weir II was revealed during a watching brief in early August 1998 when *c.* 5m long post alignment was revealed. These were recorded rapidly as the area was required for quarry access. Arrangements for a more controlled investigation were made such that a further 7m length was recorded in early September 1998. A third sample, another 16m length, was excavated later that month. The structure comprised two lines of posts forming a V-shaped planform (Figure 3): much of the second post line had been lost to quarrying operations earlier that year. The principal post

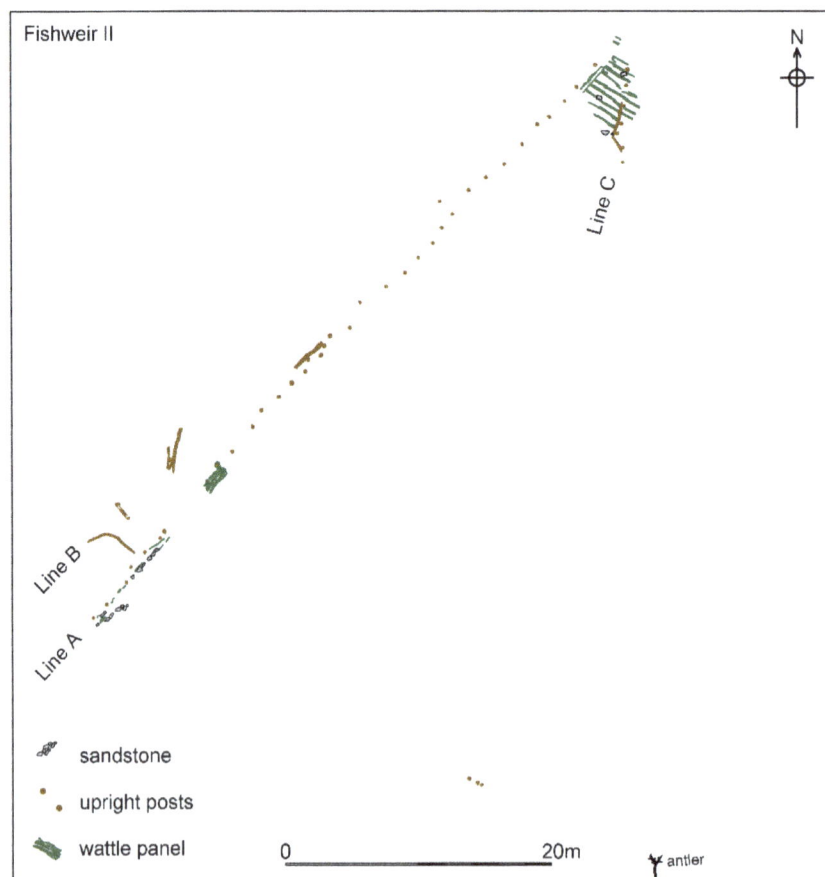

Figure 3: Plan of Fish weir II.

line A was revealed for 28m and was formed by a line of closely spaced oak piles that had been driven deep (up to 1.5m) into the contemporary river bed. Two areas where the wattle panel survived well were chosen for excavation as representative samples. Wattle panels were positioned against the upstream face of this post line, presumably tied onto the posts (though conclusive evidence was not found). Bundles of brushwood had been placed against the base of the wattle panels on the upstream face and weighed down by blocks of local sandstone. It is uncertain whether these were a later addition in response to localised scouring or part of the original design included to prevent scouring. Another possibility was that they were eel tufts (Von Brandt 1984, 138–140), such as those recorded at HL5.

Immediately to the north was an intermittent second line of posts, Line B, only recorded accurately in the westernmost 12m of the structure. Other posts were observed on this line during the quarrying but they could not be located accurately. Excavation around one of these posts revealed a horizontal timber extending towards Line A. By analogy with Fish weir I this has been interpreted as a supporting brace and tie back.

Line C was a line of closely spaced posts that formed the return arm of the fish weir. The line may have continued to the south-west joining up with some other observed posts to form a line of some 27m minimum length. Unfortunately, much of the area between the two observations was quarried

prior to any archaeological presence at the site, though the machine driver reported two or three posts from hereabouts. Limited excavation at the eastern end of the line revealed a horizontal timber and brushwood apparently placed against the upstream face of the post line. There was no evidence for the use of wattle panels in the area investigated. At the apex of Lines A and C limited excavation revealed a large wattle panel laid onto the contemporary river bed within the two post lines but also extending some way beyond them (Figure 3 and Figure 4). The panel had probably been inserted after the posts of lines A and C had been piled in position, suggested by the localised displacement of the panel's rods and sails. Three sandstone blocks lay on the surface of the panel, presumably serving to hold it in position. The wattle panel may have been introduced to prevent scour in an area subject to high flow rates caused by the funnel effect at the apex of the fish weir. It is also plausible that the panel may have provided a firm surface on which a fish trap could be placed, and/or allow a secure footing in an area of the fish trap that would have required more maintenance.

The two radiocarbon dates (Table 1) were calibrated to the Calib Rev 6.0.0 programme and rounded to nearest 10 years (Reimer *et al.* 2009). When calibrated they have an identical, albeit wide, date range in the mid-late Anglo-Saxon period. The calibrated results at 1 sigma suggest that a late 7th–8th century date might be more likely.

Figure 4: The horizontal hurdle panel (foreground) at the apex of Fish weir II and a vertical panel visible to the rear of the picture (looking northwest).

Table 1: Radiocarbon results for Fish weir II

Timber Number	Lab. Number	Structure/Description	Radiocarbon Age BP	Calibrated Results: (2 sigma, 95% probability)
1168	GrA-51551	Upright post, oak	1250 ± 35	cal AD 680–870
1171	GrA-51748	Upright post, oak	1245 ± 30	cal AD 680–870

HL 5 Fish Weir Complex (9th–10th century AD)

In 1999 further structural and artefactual evidence for fishing was found at another group of fish weirs just upstream of Fish weirs I and II. HL5 included six post-alignments (Lines A–F, Figure 5) and six hurdle-fence structures (Panel 211, 260, 261, 213, 240 and 22). The excavation results will be discussed under five headings:

• V-Shaped Fish Weir (Lines E–F)
• Post Alignment (Line D)
• Upstream Eel Trap Structure (Lines A–C and Panel 211)
• Hurdle Structure I (Panels 213, 240, 260 and 261)
• Hurdle Structure II (Panel 22).

V-Shaped Fish Weir (Lines E and F)

The V-shaped fish weir consisted of two lines of posts: Line E included 79 timber posts extending some 40m and Line F, the return, being less well-preserved, comprised five posts over 11m. At the downstream extent of the two rows the apex had been scoured away (Lines E and F, east end). There was no evidence of either scour prevention or fish catching mechanisms. Some 2.5m to the south of Line E was a second row of posts (six surviving) which are analogous to the upright posts that prevented movement in the angled bracing (Figure 34) seen at Fish weir I.

Excavation at the downstream apex showed deep scouring, and a collapse of oak piles (Figure 5, east end of Line E-F), but these appeared to be upturned pile posts rather than the principal apparatus at the apex.

Thirty-five posts from Line E-F were recorded: all were oak and 27 still had their bark. They had between 9 – 21 rings (av. 16.3 rings), they were around 100mm in diameter and most were recorded on site as slow grown. No complete lengths were recorded, although the upturned posts at the eastern end of the row were up to 2.85m long. The posts were eroded at the height of the riverbed and no wattle panelling survived. The surviving tops of the posts were between 27.25 – 28.26m AOD.

Post Alignment (Line D)

On a similar alignment to the principal post row from Line E-F was a second line of posts some 10m to the south (Line D, Figure 5. The row was more eroded than Line E-F and had been heavily scraped by machine, but was recorded as consisting of at least 27 posts. No return leader of the V was observed but a consideration at the time of excavation was that the Hurdle Structure 2 might represent its remains following scouring out of the channel. At the southwest extent of the row the posts were driven to a lesser depth, coinciding with a raising of the Holme Pierrepont gravels.

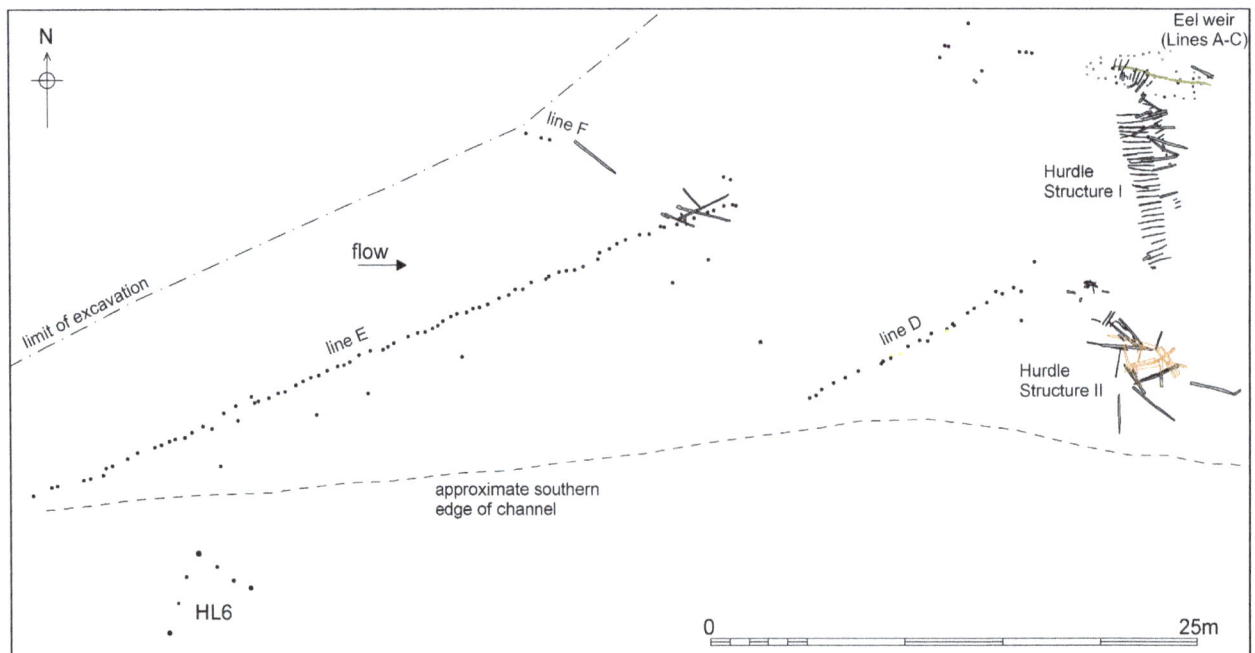

Figure 5: Plan of HL5.

Remnants of a silt/clay horizon suggest this was in the shallows of either the southern riverbank or a mid-stream island. This suggests the contemporary river was at least 20m wide (to the northernmost post of Line F).

Of the 24 posts that were recorded in detail three were noted as 'non-oak'. Nineteen still had bark attached; 4 – 19 rings were counted (mean 13.25 rings). The posts were again around 100mm in diameter. The tops of the posts were between 27.50 – 27.88m AOD.

Eel Trap Structure (Lines A–C and Panel 211)

Some 20m downstream from the V-shaped fish weir (Lines E–F) were the remains of a smaller V arrangement of posts, the probable remains of an eel trap. The arrangement of this structure was distinct from all other fish weirs observed in the quarry in that the apex of the V pointed upstream, but was also closed. It seems that the arrangement was effectively a cutwater providing a stretch of calm water to attract eels. Some eight posts formed the northern arm of the V (Line A, Figure 6). The southern arm was less clearly defined but certainly included 10 posts (Line B), possibly supported by a row of bracing posts (Line C) *c.* 1m to the south (in the manner of Fish weir I, see Figure 34), although no braces were recorded. Line C may be a predecessor to Line B although the absence of remains of hurdle panels or brushwood debris would argue against this.

Brushwood

At the base of the vertical panel the riverbed was lined with bundles of brushwood; several were clearly tied with twisted withy rope (Figure 6), but otherwise the brushwood appeared to be in loose bundles (armfuls), although still roughly aligned with post Line B. It was not clear how the bundles and loose brushwood were prevented from washing away, but there were some indications that the

bundle with a withy tie was kept in position by small pieces of roundwood passing through it and into the wattle fence. It is likely that the trap was constructed in the shallows, near the still waters of the riverbank.

Along the internal (northern) face of Line B, downstream of the line, were the remains of a vertical hurdle panel (Panel 209). No mechanism for how the panel was attached to the post was evident. The recorded segment of panel suggested it was one continuous panel 4.7m long but only the bottom 0.4m survived. At least 24 sails (uprights) were evident and most were clearly cut to a point at the lower end, to be driven in to the ground. The sails were regularly spaced at *c.* 300mm intervals. The rods (horizontals) were woven into the sails some 150mm up from the point (i.e. the sails were not deeply driven). The rods appeared to be plainly woven (in-out-in-out) in pairs, although as only *c.* 7–8 layers of rods survived, this was not replicated with certainty. The bottom tips of the sails of the panel clearly rose towards the apex of the V, with the western end being some 0.5m higher than the east, perhaps suggesting the apex was near the riverbank.

It has been suggested that the use of brushwood against wattle fences would have made them fish-tight, possibly added after localized scouring had occurred (Losco-Bradley and Salisbury 1979, 19). An alternative, and not necessarily mutually exclusive purpose, is suggested by one of the brushwood bundles (T208) adjacent to SF22 (Figure 6). Excavation revealed a sheep metapodial lodged within the brushwood. It would appear that this was bait for an eel tuft i.e. brushwood bundles used as artificial shelters for fish, exploiting the hiding behaviour of species such as eels, burbot and lampreys (Von Brandt 1984, 138–140). In Germany eel tufts were brushwood bundles tied together like broom heads and submerged. The bundles would be carefully lifted, with a scoop net under the brushwood, or quickly thrown into the boat before any fish escaped (*ibid*).

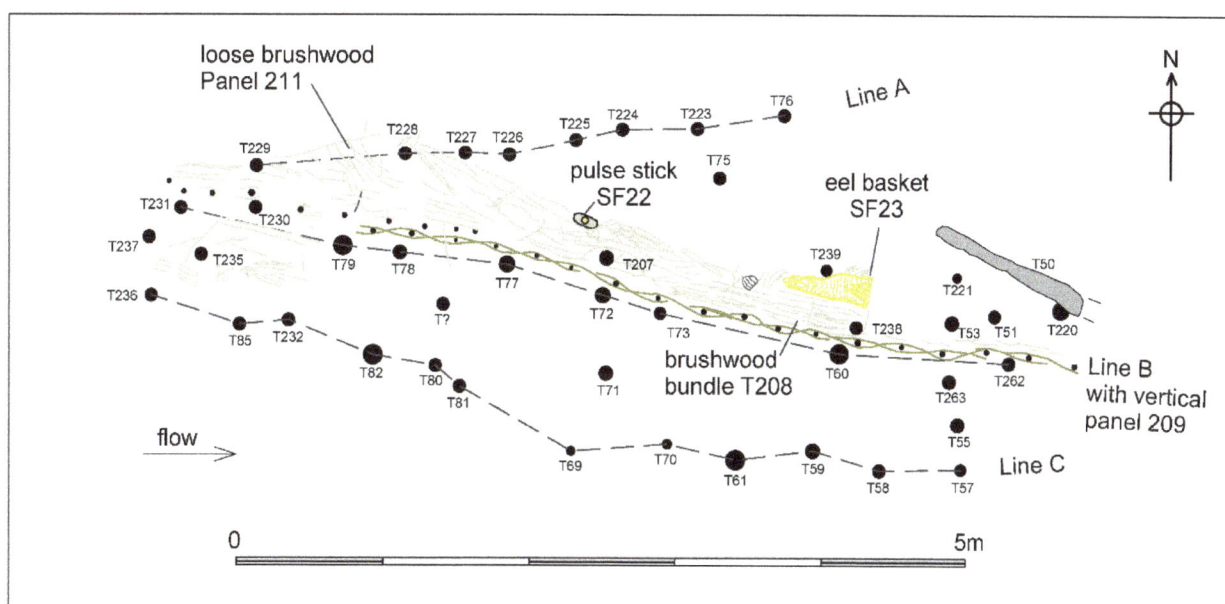

Figure 6: The HL5 eel trap structure with surviving eel basket and eel tufts (e.g. brushwood bundle T208).

Eel Basket SF23

Nestled in silt between the brushwood bundle T208 and an upright Post 239 were the remains of a small but remarkably well-preserved wicker eel catching basket (SF23, Figure 6 and Figure 7). Possibly once secured to Post 239 (although no ties were observed) the basket was held in place by a vertical stake at its narrow end. It had been sectioned longitudinally during previous clearance works (there was evidence for blade tooth marks in the area at this level – the supervised stripping was undertaken with a flat blade). Ironically, the sectioning of the basket allowed its form to be seen clearly. It was bottle-shaped with an in-turned cone entrance which had an unfinished opening of loose wicker, forming an effective non-return valve. The narrow opening at the other end was secured by a wooden stopper, apparently held in place by a piece of withy.

The basket was 600mm long by 230mm wide at widest and was made with an estimated 20+ sails and 132+ rods, plainly woven (single withies woven alternately in-out-in-out). The basket was made of un-split willow with its bark still attached. The longitudinal stakes were from two year old willow, harvested in the autumn or winter. The weft rods used in the weave were from one year old willow.

Peter Carter (pers. comm.), an eel basket maker from The Fens, believed it is likely that the basket was made by weaving around a wooden frame or mould, holding an odd number of warp stakes (Figure 8). When the weaving was *c.* 200mm deep, (the internal funnel at the mouth of the basket) the stakes would then have been bent backwards in a U-turn, to form the cone shape of the body of the basket (Figure 9). The basket would have been placed mouth downwards, forming a stable base from which to weave the body of the basket. The weft was woven as a continuous spiralling circuit, being beaten down after each circuit, until the cone was drawn to a close at the bung end

The wicker trap was placed with its entrance facing downstream, a position typical of yellow eel traps exploiting their behaviour to swim upstream tracing the scent of their food (Sinha and Jones 1975, fig 8.3).

Although only one basket was identified a number of posts lay within the V which were not obviously associated with the structure of the V. These may have had other structural functions but may equally have anchored further traps (Posts 51. 53, 75, 207, 220, 221, 230 and 238, Figure 6). Posts 263, 55, 71, 235 and 237, (lying between Lines B and C) may have served a similar function.

Figure 7: Eel Basket SF23 with downstream facing 'non-return valve' to the left and plug to the right (i.e. the river flows from right to left). The basket was approximately 600mm long by 200mm wide at the mouth.

Figure 8: Mould used to shape the funnel of an eel basket.

Figure 10: Pulse stick.

Figure 11: Reverse face of pulse stick.

Small Find 22

0   300mm

Figure 12: Drawing of Pulse Stick SF22 showing mechanism for attaching a handle and the location of cut marks on both face.

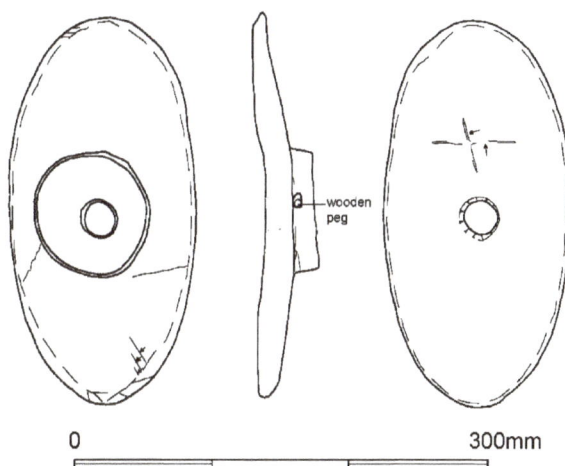

Figure 9: Right, the withy strakes bent back to form the body of the basket.

Pulse Stick Head SF22

Immediately upstream of the eel basket and resting against a brushwood bundle was an enigmatic wooden artefact (Figure 10, Figure 11 and Figure 12). The object was an oval-shaped plank of wood, 270mm long by 136 wide and generally 19mm thick (tapering at the edges). Through the centre of the object was a circular hole 25mm in diameter, but just-off perpendicular to the flat face of the object. Any handle driven through the object would not quite have been at 90°.

On one face of the object, the wood had been left to a thickness of 40mm in a ring around the central hole. On the surface of the ring concentric marks were visible (Figure 10) as though the ring had been turned on a lathe. In the side of the ring was a small perforation (7mm diameter) with the remains of a wooden dowel peg in the hole. The hole and peg were evidently to fasten a handle. It was generally water-worn and smooth but small cut marks from a blade at least 40mm wide were still visible. On the reverse face to the 'raised ring' the object was again completely smooth except for an 'X' cut with a 60mm wide blade.

The object was originally reported as the head of a pulse stick (Cooper 2003), a tool used for driving fish into nets and traps, or to prevent them escaping before a net is closed (Von Brandt 1984, 123–4). In Germany pulse sticks are used to this day to frighten eels into trammel nets (*ibid.*). Those described by Von Brandt have hemispherical heads attached to long handles (rather like an elongated sink plunger) and moved up and down rhythmically in the water. The position of the pulse stick at HL5, resting against one of the tied bundles, might suggest that the eels were kept inside the bundles by scaring them with the pulse stick. However, another possibility is that it is the head of a quant pole used to brace the shoulder or chest when moving a boat by quanting (Richard Darrah, pers. comm.). A parsimonious interpretation might be that it is part of a composite tool.

Wooden Bowl Fragment SF25

A fragment of a finely turned wooden bowl was recovered from this general area (Figure 13). The bowl was lathe turned. The body-walls were *c.* 5mm thick, tapering to about 3mm at the rim. The outer surface was turned smooth, although two contrasting small grooves cut into the base of the neck suggest it was decorated. Its similarity to the more complete SF29 (Figure 28) suggests this was also a cup, although an insufficient amount of rim survived to allow an estimation of the rim diameter.

Hurdle Structure I (Panels 213, 240, 260 and 261)

Hurdle Structure I consisted of a probable three rows of collapsed hurdle fencing (Panel 240, Panel 213 and the amalgamated Panels 260/261) and a number of collapsed support posts. The three panels were staggered (240 furthest south, then 213 and 260/1 furthest north and curving). All were in various states of collapse.

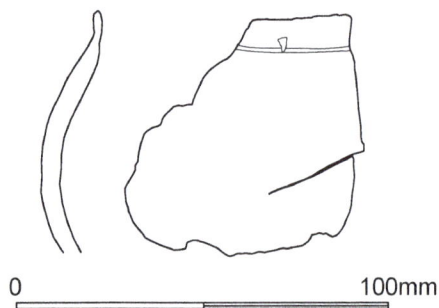

Panel 240

The wattle fence T240 was 8m long and 1.35m high and had survived by being buried in a gravel and silt filled scour feature (Figure 14 – Figure 16). Despite good overall preservation both extremes of the fence had rotted away, though a single rod was observed passing around the most southerly upright suggesting it was a terminal.

The fence consisted of 29 sails (uprights): mostly single rods but at least six sails were made of pairs. Each was up to 1.22m long and spaced at roughly 300–400mm intervals (slightly more closely spaced towards the middle). The rods had been woven in a fanned pattern so that the lowermost were horizontal gradually fanning to diagonal. The diagonal design makes the panel stronger so that it is less likely to lift off the top. The very top rows were paired with two rods woven simultaneously to give a stronger grip. The rest were laid singly. The absence of paired rods at the bottom of the fence suggests it was built *in situ* (Tabor, 2000).

Behind wattle fence T240, approximately 1m to the east, was another parallel length of collapsed wattle fence (recorded as three separate elements T213, T260 and T261). The northern end of the fence (Panel 260/261) was both tilting (pushed-over with the flow) and curving in plan. The partially exposed southerly section (recorded as Panel 213), was straight in plan, at least 3.60m long by at least 0.90m tall and appeared to be plainly woven with both single rods and sails

Between the two rows of fence lines eight timber posts were observed (Figure 15 and Figure 17) that were notably larger than the posts that supported the wattle fencing. These large posts appeared to be deliberately set at 45° and crossed each other, presumably to both brace the fences from downstream movement and to hold the two lines a set distance apart. Five posts had their pointed ends upstream/west (Posts 62, 63, 128, 216 and 219) and five downstream (Posts 65, 214, 215, 217 and 218). One of the braces passed through the wattle Panel 213.

Figure 13: Finely turned wooden bowl fragment SF25. The scrape to the bottom left is modern trowel damage.

Figure 14: Collapsed hurdle fence Panel 240, looking east.

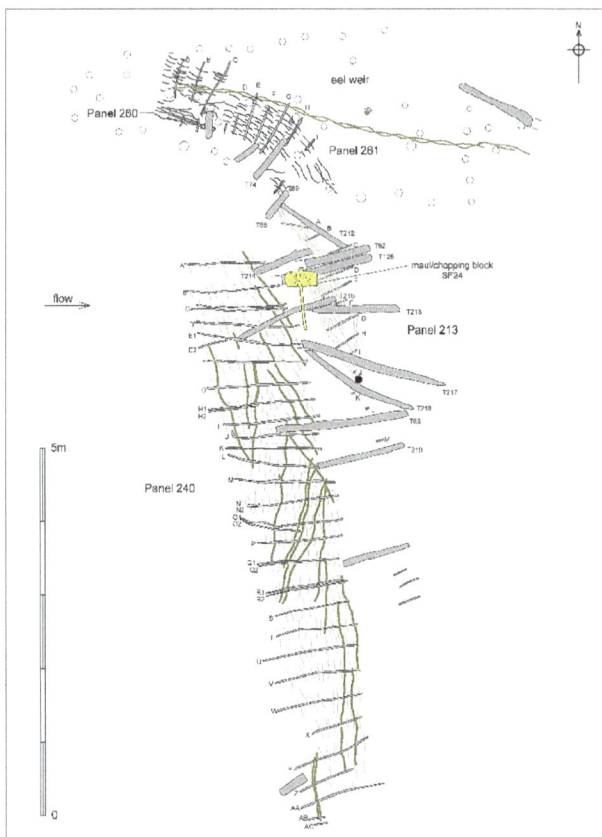

Figure 15: Hurdle Structure I (Panels 240, 213 and 260) and the faint outline of the eel trap structure to the north.

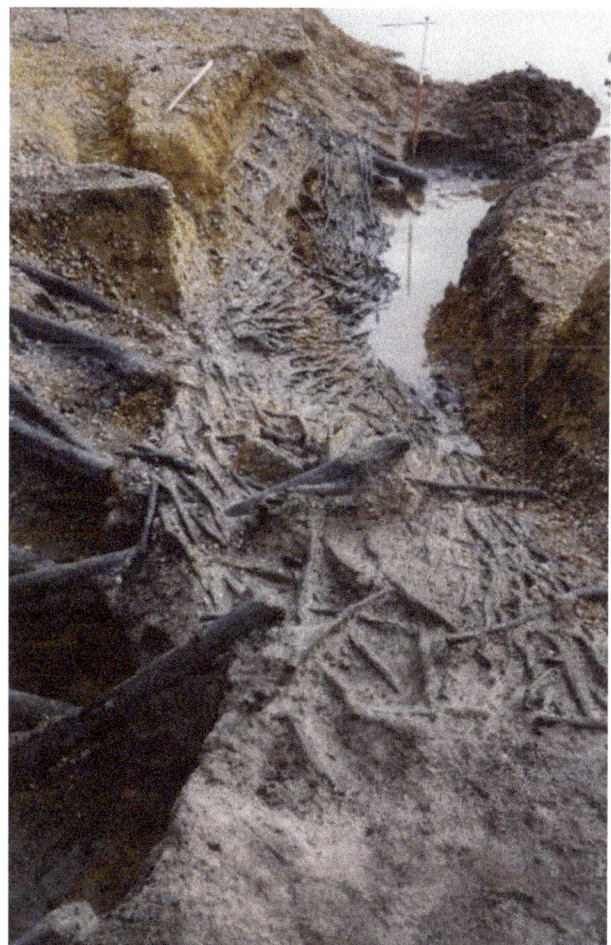

Figure 16: Panel 240, looking south.

Wooden Maul/Chopping Block SF24

The structure appears to be a double row of fences that were cross-braced. It is conceivable that the fences formed a crib, possibly infilled with gravel to form a weir, although Peter Carter (pers. comm.) has suggested that it was likely to be a long double fence structure forming a funnel that would have been netted at its end, to catch silver eels on their seaward migration.

Lying directly on top of two of the cross-brace timbers behind Panel 240 (Figure 15, Figure 18) was an unusual mallet-shaped timber artefact (SF24). It had a cylindrical head (380mm x 180mm diameter) and was jointed to a haft (840mm long by 40mm diameter). The haft was slightly tapered to fit into a hole in the head and could be clearly

Figure 17: Bracing behind Panel 240, looking south. Panel 213 is to the left of the photo.

Figure 18: Excavation of the wooden maul/chopping block.

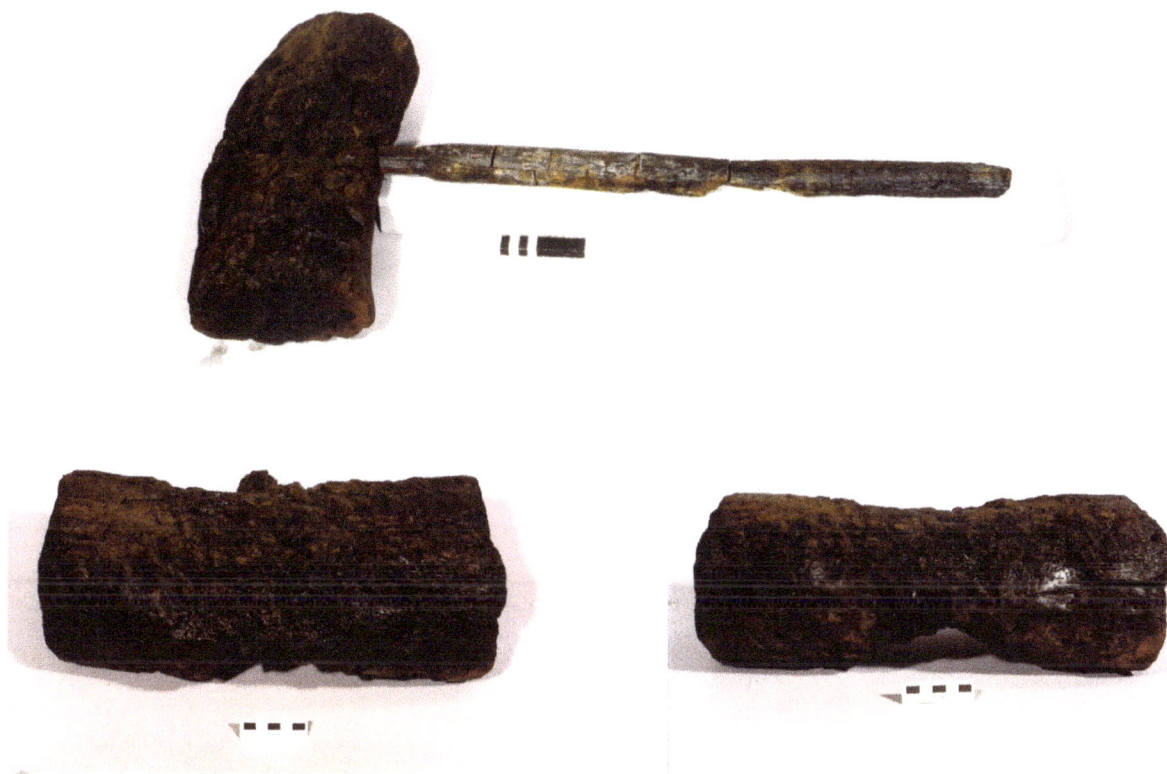

Figure 19: Three views of the maul/chopping block

seen to emerge on the other side. There was no evidence for any 'fixing' to stop the haft coming away from the head: it was merely jammed in. Both the head and shaft were willow/poplar.

Although mallet-like in shape, the narrow diameter of the haft suggests it would not have been practicable to have used this implement to hammer with. The head had evidence on both sides for multiple chop-marks (Figures 19–21). The chop marks were so numerous that the cylinder had become 'waisted' towards the centre and the chop-marks difficult to distinguish. No full blade profiles were visible but at least one blade was over 60mm wide. While all faces of the head had been subjected to chops the two ends were comparatively unscathed: indentations would be expected if the object had been used as a hammer. It seems likely that the object was a 'chopping block', the 'haft' merely being a handle to hold the chopping board steady and to carry it.

Most fish and/or eels would be stored live when first caught (Peter Carter, pers. comm.) and would not have been cut up on site, but Tabor (2000, re-drawn in this volume, below) illustrates a wooden post labelled 'chopping block to cut the ends of willows for on site hurdle making' in an illustration of how to construct a hurdle panel. A chopping block may also have been used to cut meat to bait the traps.

Hurdle Structure II (Panel 22 and Timbers Below)

A few metres to the south of Hurdle Structure I was a third group of hurdle panels and a jumble of posts. The area was

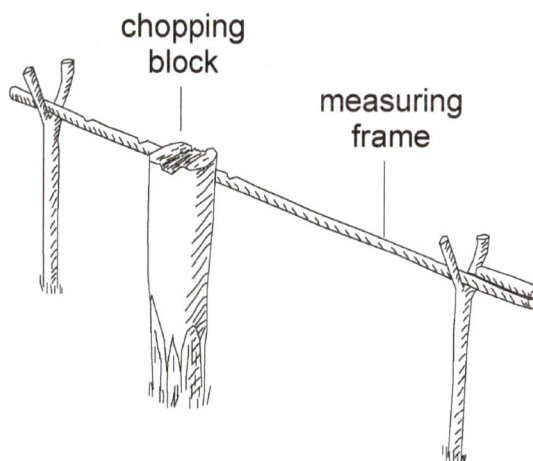

Figure 20: Chopping block as part of hurdle-making apparatus (re-drawn from Tabor 2000, Fig. 13.18, 119).

waterlogged and it was only possible to glimpse much of the structure with the aid of a pump. The earliest phase of collapsed posts is illustrated in Figures 22 and 24. It consisted of at least 11 dislodged pile posts and numerous brushwood fragments. The posts ranged from 0.6m to 2.8m long, 900 – 160mm in diameter, whole oak timbers and cut to a point at one end (i.e. pile driven). The points were not aligned and appeared to demonstrate the calamitous collapse of a structure, possibly the corresponding leader to a V-shaped weir with post line D.

Lying directly on top of the posts and probably once associated with them were the remains of a horizontal hurdle panel together with further scattered uprights (Figures 23, 25–27). The panel was 3.4m wide, by nearly 2m high. At

Small Find 24

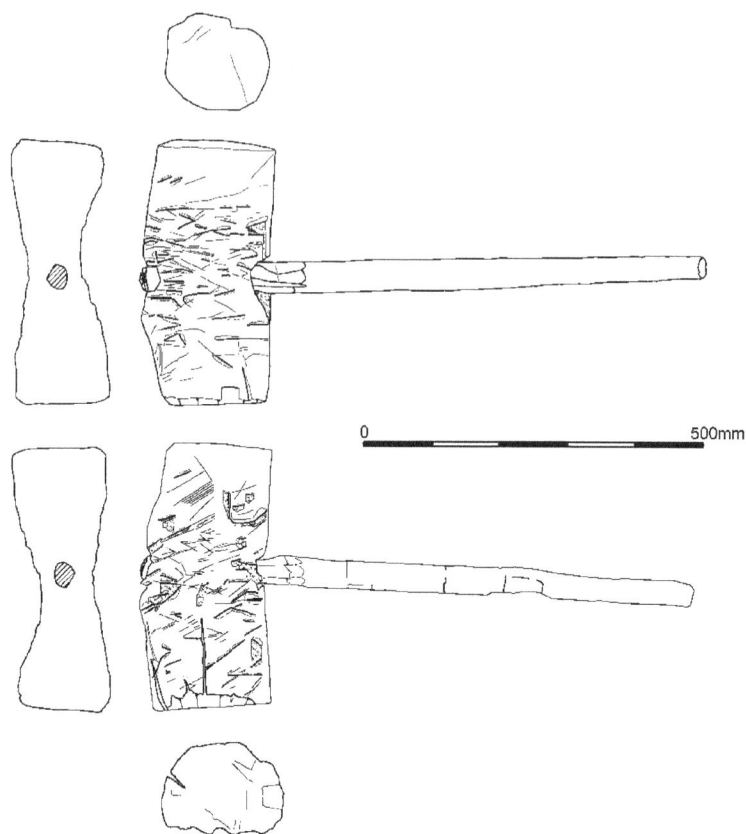

Figure 21: Maul SF24. Nb the abundance of cut marks on the 'head', while the end faces were comparatively unscathed.

Figure 22: Hurdle Structure II; the collection of collapsed posts lying below Panel 22.

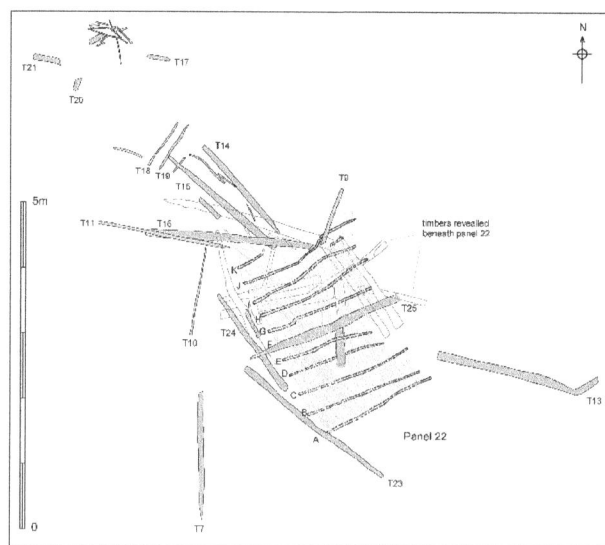

Figure 23: Hurdle Structure II; plan of Panel 22 with further posts, below the water table, visible below.

the southern end of the panel the rods were clearly wrapped around the last upright (i.e. a finished end to the panel) although the northern end was not distinguished.

Panel 22 consisted of 11 upright sails (A-K, Figure 23) and *c.* 33 pairs of rods, plainly woven (in-out-in-out). Tabor

(2000) states that sheep hurdles are usually 1.8m long by 1m high, with 10 uprights, the maximum size for a panel that is regularly moved. It is suggested that Panel 22 was likely to have been made *in situ*, during the summer months when low river level would have allowed construction work on the river bed. The rods in Panel 22 were woven straight across for the top and bottom 5 or so rows, but woven diagonally across the centre, presumably to create

Figure 24: Hurdle Structure II, earliest phase of posts.

Figure 25: Hurdle Panel 22, looking south.

cross-bracing and to give the panel greater strength (Figure 23).

A further 12 upright posts were found in association with the panel. Post 25 appeared to be woven in to the panel with the point of the post pointing westward. Post 12 may have been a brace to Post 25. If the panel was once upright it is likely that all these posts may once have supported the hurdle panel and the structure may have been a continuation of Hurdle Structure I or the remains of a corresponding leader to post line D.

To the south of Hurdle Structure II the gravels became increasingly waterlogged and no further timbers were observed. It is presumed that any further structures are likely to have been destroyed as the river migrated southwards.

Wooden Bowl Fragment SF29

A small, near-complete wooden bowl or cup was recovered from a sand deposit adjacent to wattle Panel 22 (Figure

Figure 26: Hurdle Panel 22, looking north.

23; Figures 28–29). The bowl was made from hand-turned wood and although irregular in profile it was roughly 60mm diameter across the base, 104mm diameter at its widest point and 80mm wide at the rim. The walls of the

Figure 27: Detail of Panel 22, looking west.

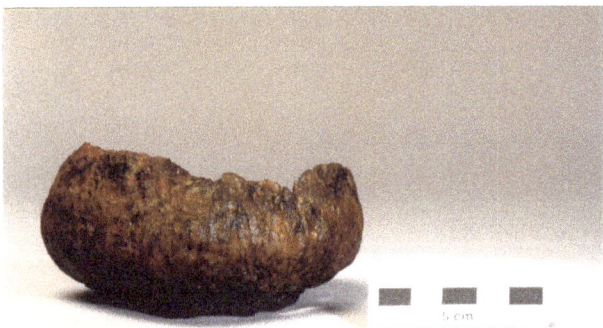

Figure 28: Wooden Bowl fragment SF29 from the Hurdle Structure II area.

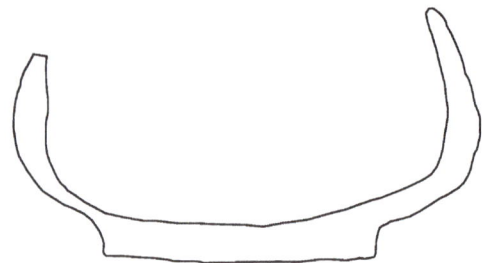

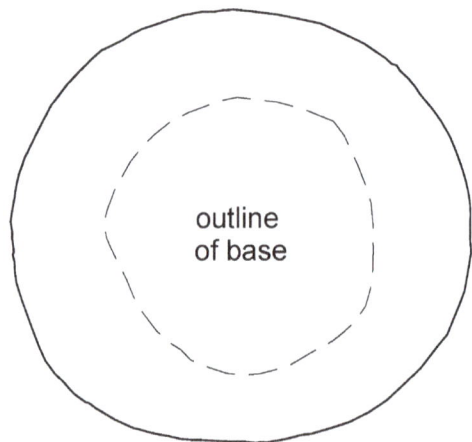

Figure 29: Wooden Bowl SF29.

Table 2: Radiocarbon results from HL5 structures

Timber Number	Lab. Number	Structure/Description	Radiocarbon Age BP	Calibrated Results: (2 sigma, 95% probability)
60	GrA-51543	Line B, oak post	1150 ± 30	cal AD 780–790 cal AD 800–970
72	GrA-51474	Line B, oak post	1105 ± 30	cal AD 890–1010
96	GrA51545	Line D, oak post	1205 ± 30	cal AD 690–700 cal AD 710–750 cal AD 760–890
99	GrA-51547	Line D, oak post	1155 ± 30	cal AD 780–790 cal AD 800–970
126	GrA-51548	Line E, oak post	1115 ± 30	cal AD 870–1010
145	GrA-51549	Line E, oak post	1090 ± 70	cal AD 890–1010

bowl were again uneven and varied between 3mm and 8mm thick. It was not quite flat across the base.

The six radiocarbon determinations (Table 2) were calibrated to the Calib Rev 6.0.0 programme and rounded to nearest 10 years (Reimer *et al.* 2009). The dates are broadly similar though, when considering the most probable 1 sigma determinations it is possible that the post lines B and E are 10th century but the post line D is 9th century. The possibility that line D is the surviving leader on the landward side of a part destroyed V-shaped fish weir may imply that the more complete fish weir (lines E and F) was a direct replacement.

Fish Weir I (Mid 11th–Mid 12th Century AD)

Excavation of a post alignment located during the overburden stripping in March 1998 revealed a row of 51 posts, on a north-west to south-east alignment, extending over 20m (Figures 30–31). The alignment, running obliquely across silt-clay palaeochannel remains (the riverbed), suggested that the structure was a fish weir (Fish

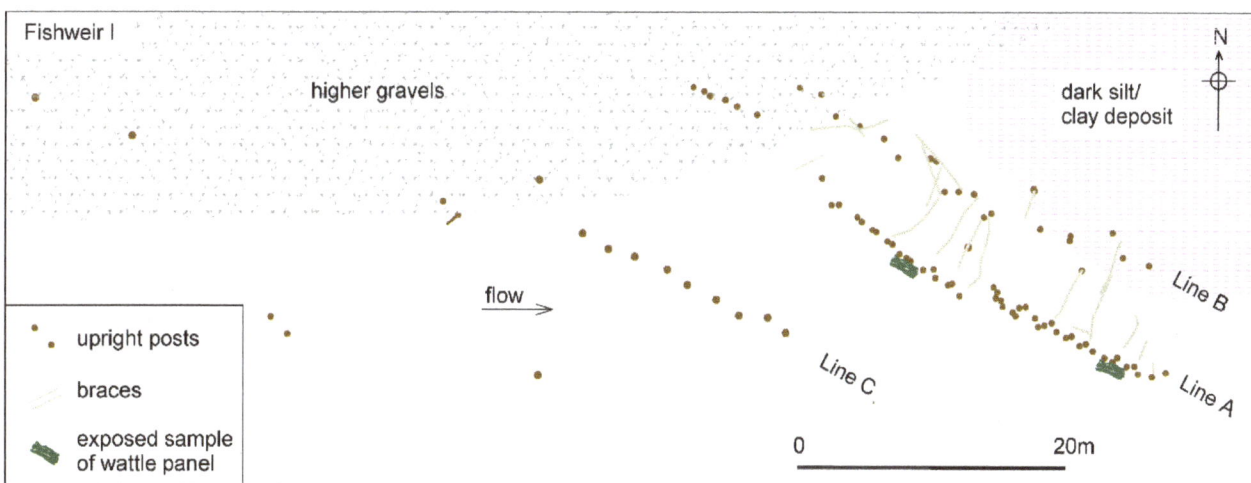

Figure 30: Plan of Fish weir I.

Figure 31: Fish weir I, Line A.

Figure 32: Fish weir I, Line B.

weir I) rather than a riverside structure. At its north-western extent the posts were only driven to a shallow depth as they ran into the riverbank, indicating a genuine limit to the structure. The south-eastern extent of the row ran under a peninsular of gravel reserved to site the quarry drainage pump and could not be examined.

The posts lying within the river (i.e. excluding the posts driven to a shallow depth, timbers 46–51) were all 1.5–2m

long and were driven into the river gravels to a depth of *c.* 1m (Figure 30, Line A). Wattle panels were then positioned against the upstream face of this post line (Figures 33–34). Two well-preserved areas of wattle panelling (sections 1:2 and 5:1) were then examined in detail. The panelling survived up to a height of 1.40m but the length of each panel could not be determined. The panels appeared to have been woven with alternate single and double uprights ('sails') with plainly woven horizontals ('rods'). There was

Figure 33: One of the exposed samples of hurdle panels, Fish weir I, Line A.

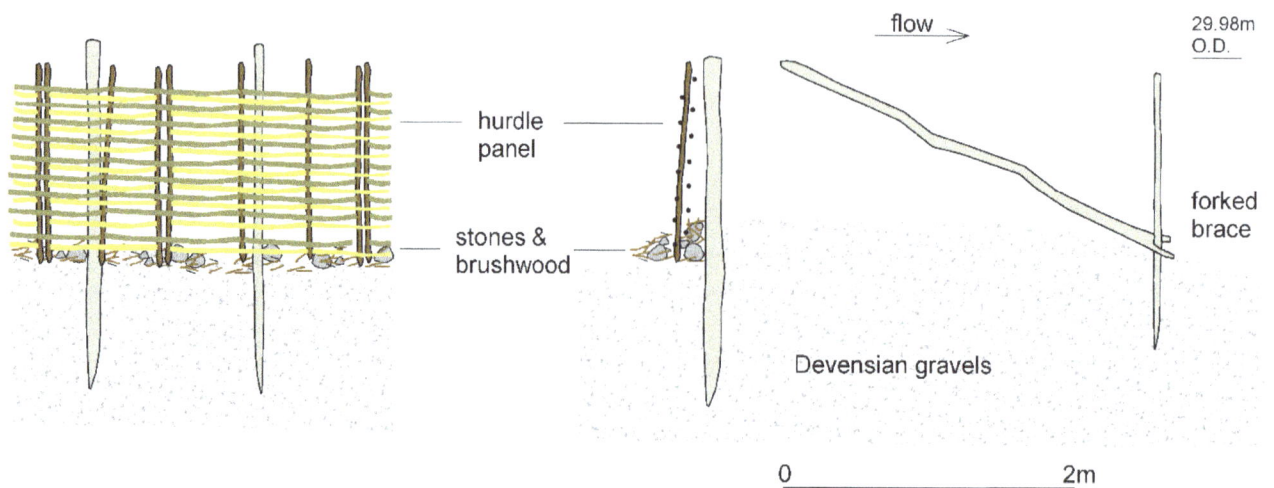

Figure 34: Measured sketch drawing showing: left, the construction of one of the recorded panel's segments, right, how the hurdle panels rested against Line A, which was supported by bracing which was 'pinned' in place by a second row of posts (Line B) (Fig. 30).

some evidence to suggest that bundles of brushwood were then placed against the base of panels and possibly staked to the riverbed with roundwood pegs.

Nearly one-third of the timbers in the main post row were supported by angled bracing timbers (Figure 32). All the bracing timbers were made up of knotty, twisted timbers (side branches) and were up to 3m long, set at an angle of approximately 45°. No joint connecting the brace timbers to the uprights survived as they were above the level that had remained waterlogged. The base of all the exposed brace ends included a fork at the point at which a side branch had been left attached. Each of these forks was then stopped against an upright post, preventing movement in the brace. Some 22 of such brace-supporting posts were observed.

Some 5m to the south-west of the fish weir a second row of posts, on a similar alignment to Fish weir I, was noted (Figure 30, Line C). Ten posts were uncovered over some 11m, all of which were sampled. six of the posts were measured and were between 0.73m and 1.70m long, noticeably shorter than Lines A and B. It seems probable that Line C was the remains of a possibly earlier fish weir.

A total of 11 other posts was also noted in the southern extent of Phase 5 of the quarry. All were located with a total station and where possible the timbers were sampled.

A total of 102 timbers and 32 wattle rods was sampled. Six timbers were examined and indicated that oak, willow/ poplar and alder/hazel were all used. All were from young trees (up to 30 rings) with only a small diameter (*c.* 150mm). The six samples have all been radiocarbon dated and calibrated to the Calib Rev 6.0.0 programme and rounded to nearest 10 years (Reimer *et al.* 2009).

The radiocarbon results indicate that Fish weir I was constructed in the early medieval period (Table 3). The three timbers that have a certain association with the fish weir (1016, 1049 and 1062) have a wide calibrated radiocarbon range but only overlap from the mid 11th to mid 12th century. Panel 1114 is erroneously old, and is

dismissed as an anomalous date. The date ranges of the two single posts (1002 and 1134) would suggest that they were also felled within the same period as Fishweir I.

Discussion of Fish Weirs

The three fish weir sites are all examples of what the Anglo-Saxons termed *haecwera*, hedge weirs (Seebohm 1905, 153). The construction methods were quite similar with the close-set oak piles being driven to a depth of 0.7–1.7m deep. The posts were braced with canted timbers with forked bases that allowed them to be anchored by a secondary, downstream line of piles. Attached to the upstream side were wattle panels made as pre-fabricated hurdles. Brushwood was often found at the base of the panels, sometimes with clear evidence for being tied bundles, and may have been intended to make the fences fish-tight. However, the brushwood could also have been used as eel tufts to lure yellow eels. The apex or eye of Quarry Phase 5 Fish Weir II had an integral horizontal wattle panel used to armour the river bed in an area subject to bed scour. There are a few gaps along the principal lines of the fish weirs and these may be occasional lost posts or, feasibly, gaps in which secondary traps such as baskets or nets were placed.

One of the subsidiary structures at HL5 would appear to have been constructed for the trapping of yellow eels. Wattle hedges were placed to act as a breakwater and provide a secluded stretch of channel, conditions that would have attracted yellow eels. Eel traps in the form of small baskets and baited brushwood bundles were placed in the slack waters. The traps would probably have been serviced from small boats (Figure 35).

Salisbury reported some forty-three examples of possible fish weirs from the Hemington Quarry extraction from 1985–1994 (Salisbury and Brown 2009). The recording capabilities in a working quarry were very difficult such that little structural detail could be recorded. Indeed, the limited observations of many structures, fragments of post alignments within a working tranche of the quarry,

Table 3: Radiocarbon results from Fish weir I

Timber Number	Lab. Number	Structure/Description	Radiocarbon Age BP	Calibrated Results: (2 sigma, 95% probability)
1002	Beta-119654	Upright post, oak, *c.* 20m south of Fish weir I	1050 ± 50	cal AD 880-1050 cal AD 1090–1120 cal AD 1140–1150
1016	Beta-119655	Upright post, willow/poplar, from Fish weir I	970 ± 60	cal AD 970–1210
1049	Beta-119656	Upright post, alder/hazel, from Fish weir I	1010 ± 60	cal AD 890–1160
1062	Beta-119657	Upright post, oak, at base of brace, Fish weir I	870 ± 60	cal AD 1040- 1260
1114	Beta-119658	Wattle rod, willow/poplar (section 5:1)	1330 ± 70	cal AD 600–880
1134	Beta-119659	Upright post, willow/poplar, from row 5m west of Fish weir I	960 ± 70	cal AD 900–920 cal AD 970–1220

Figure 35: Victorian print (c. 1880) of setting eel traps from the Amoret Tanner Collection.

means that it is possible that some structures could have been bank revetments or jetties rather than fish weirs. However, one structure, PL 50/52, was recorded in some detail by Salisbury and a team of local volunteers. A V-shaped arrangement of posts, the fish weir leaders, was traced across the quarry with arms of 16m and 32m. The downstream apex or 'eye' indicates that it was designed to catch silver eels on their downstream migration to the sea, ultimately to the Sargasso Sea.

Some 398 posts were recorded from the old quarry (ibid.) comprising species of oak (61.8%), alder (11%), hazel (10.5%), holly (10.3%), birch (2.0%), maple (1.5%), willow (1.3%), hawthorn (1.0%), rowan (0.7%) and a little ash and elder (0.2%). The posts supported wattle or brushwood fences. Where wattle panels were used the species was exclusively hazel while *in situ* wattling was of oak, birch, hazel, rowan, willow, holly, alder and cherry. Analysis of the timber from HL5 showed that the posts were almost exclusively oak while the hurdles were constructed from willow and hazel (Radini, below). The majority of the oaks were felled in the winter but the occasional inclusion of summer-felled timber was noted. It can be suggested that the weirs were constructed in the summer when the Trent was at its lowest. The proportions of winter:summer felling is best interpreted as the summer construction with a majority of stored timber with shortfalls made up by summer-felled timber. Archbishop Wulfstan in the early

11th century described the summer construction of fish weirs on the well-run estate (Liebermann 1903–1916).

In addition to the Anglo-Saxon and medieval structures at the Colwick Quarry reported in the seminal papers of Losco-Bradley and Salisbury (1979) and Salisbury (1981) the Trent has provided other examples of fish weirs of hedge weir type. A watching brief at Swarkestone Quarry revealed a large V-shaped structure with remarkable similarities to the Hemington Quarry structures (Knight *et al.* 2007). The V-shaped structure was some 12m long with a downstream apex. Each arm comprised a double row of posts, the downstream rows A and D likely to be supports for canted braces as seen at Hemington Quarry with the fish weirs reported here. The posts were close-set some 0.5–0.75m apart and were entirely of oak. There were no signs of vertical wattle panels but these may have been removed at the end of a fishing season. Another reported fish weir was found at Alvaston comprising two parallel lines of posts (Rayner 2004). There is an associated radiocarbon date of Cal AD 1000–1250 (920 ± 60 BP).

3

Settlement (HL 4)

The intermittent watching brief precluded the monitoring of the initial sub-soil strip. South of the Tipnall Bank the sand and gravels exposed were a high remnant of the Holme Pierrepont terrace. The upper levels were slightly over-stripped leading to the partial loss of some features including part of a roundhouse. South of the latter the machining was undertaken under archaeological supervision. The western zone was subject to full excavation. The eastern zone was subject to rescue recording with exposed features planned with Total Station.

Bronze Age Roundhouse

An arc of post-holes is interpreted as part of a late Bronze Age roundhouse (Figure 36). There is an apparent entrance to the south-east evident from two pairs of post-holes with a flared planform. It is plausible that a number of the unphased pits may be contemporary, with the apparent 4-post structure to the south being a good contender.

Anglo-Saxon Structures

Two sub-square post-built structures and a dense cluster of pits and post-holes are thought to be Anglo-Saxon (Figure 36). Despite total excavation of the pits and post-holes finds recovery was extremely low. Three pits produced pottery but only one produced any significant amount – *c.* 30 pieces from one vessel provisionally dated to the earlier Anglo-Saxon period (spot dating on discovery – the pottery was not available at the time of analysis). This pit also produced a number of fire-cracked pebbles and charcoal fragments. Another pit from which pottery was recovered also contained several fragments of fired clay and charcoal. A further pit contained flecks of burnt clay, fire-cracked stones and a flint implement (notched flake/denticulate).

The western structure had been built with close-set posts with a wide eastern entrance (Figure 37). The close spacing is reminiscent of some examples from Mucking (Hamerow 1993). While it is possible that the structure is a fenced enclosure its scale and use of large timbers seems more to suggest a sub-square building. The chamfered corners are a common feature of Anglo-Saxon buildings. The

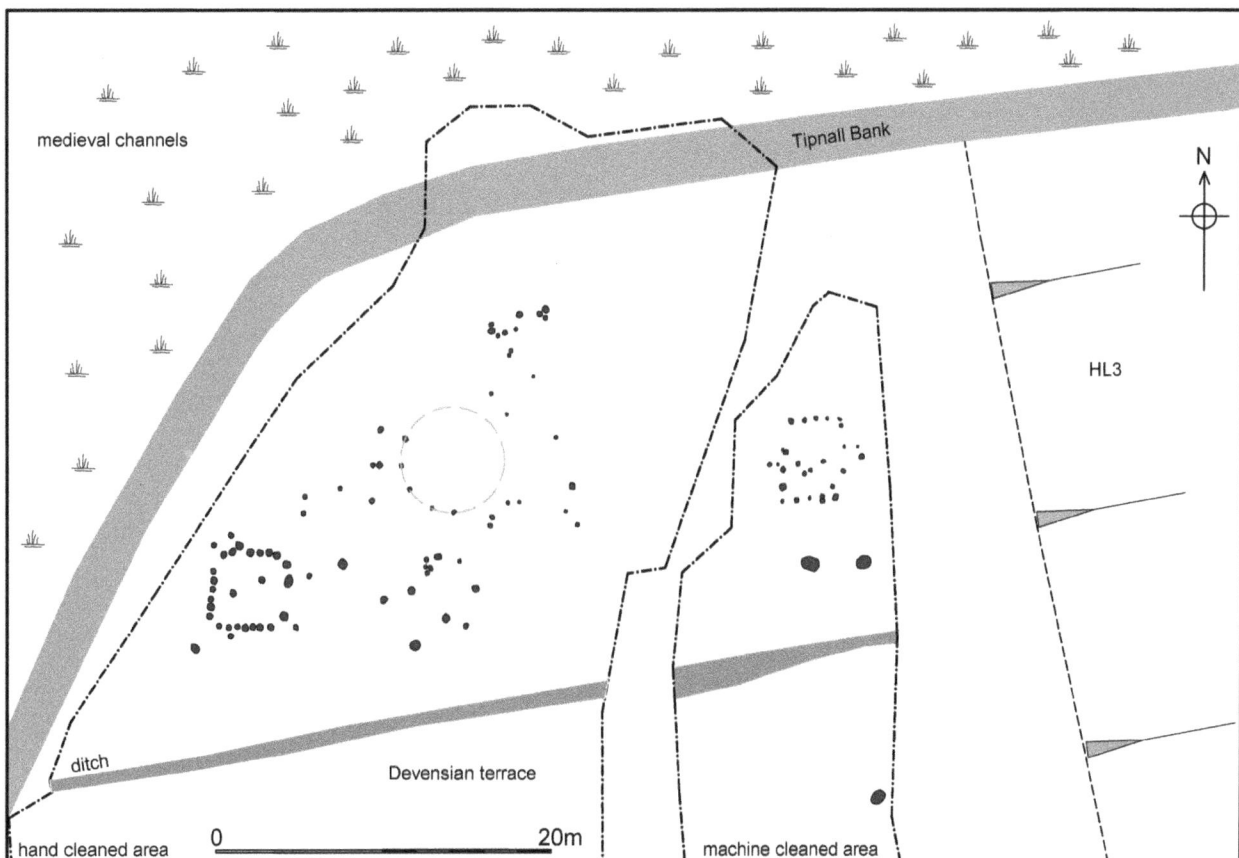

Figure 36: HL4 post-hole structures.

Figure 37: Square post-hole structure from HL4.

sides of such are likely to have been joined with dragon ties (diagonal timbers linking the wall plates). This could have supported a pyramidal roof with the rafters coming down onto the dragon ties (Mark Gardiner pers. comm.). A magnetic susceptibility survey failed to show any evidence for a hearth or internal divisions. However, two 'hot spots' were recorded which corresponded with natural features. It is possible that the entrance 'hot spot' was enhanced by the effects of trampling in the area (Adrian Butler pers. comm.).

The eastern building was recorded in a rescue situation such that we cannot be certain if the planform was complete. It was of comparable size to the western structure but the posts were smaller, not so close set and there were corner posts.

Early Medieval Ditch

Immediately south of the latter features was a ditch on the same alignment as the medieval ridge and furrow system and was parallel with the northern section of Tipnall Bank. However, it extended beneath Tipnall Bank, indicating that it is earlier than this section of the earthwork. A single sherd from the ditch fill is of early medieval date.

Discussion of Settlement Sites

The HL4 features were all located on the high terrace gravels and as such would not be prone to flooding. A similar riverside location was exploited during the Bronze

Age and Anglo-Saxon periods at the site of Willows Farm, Castle Donington (Coward and Ripper 1999). The two Anglo-Saxon structures have been reported as bothies, that is artisan workshops, probably associated with fishing and/ or harvesting (Cooper 2003). However, Mark Gardiner (pers. comm.) has suggested another possible function as processing and smoke houses for fish. The mass haul of eels in the autumn would have required some means of preservation, and drying or salting seem unlikely methods: the nearest sources of salt in Cheshire and Lincolnshire are some distance away. There is some support for the smoking interpretation in the recovery of charcoal and fire cracked stones from the site. One can especially envisage the western structure as a smoke house, its roof architecture providing ideal supports for hanging fish, especially eels. Smoked eels are a delicacy in parts of Europe today (Anita Radini pers. comm.).

4

The Stone Weir HL12 (Early 12th Century)

Introduction

The HL12 weir was located in a palaeochannel of the River Trent (Figure 1), to the south of the modern river course (Figure 2), in a stretch of the river that included the mill dam excavated in 1985 (Clay and Salisbury 1990), the Hemington Bridges found in 1993 (Ripper and Cooper 2009) and numerous other riverine structures and artefacts (Cooper 2003; Salisbury and Brown 2009). The meander belt of the Trent was active from the 8th to the 13th centuries, but was then deeply buried beneath sand and gravel deposited by the river.

The weir was observed over 65m but, as a consequence of ancient river migration and modern quarrying, it was not possible to distinguish the original banks of the river. It was clear that the southern end of the weir was upstream and was funnelling water towards a gap at the northern end. The flow direction indicated in Figure 3 is an approximation. The modern Trent is *c.* 40m wide which is not dissimilar to the width indicated by the early 12th century bridge less than 1km to the east of the weir (Ripper and Darrah 2009, Fig.10).

HL12 was a large submerged dam or weir formed by two parallel lines of oak piles supporting wattle sheeting (Figure 38). The riverbed between the posts was also lined, either with horizontal wattle sheeting or bundles of brushwood. This framework formed a large crib which was then filled with blocks of local sandstone and Millstone Grit (Figure 39). At the northern end was a V-shaped arrangement of posts and baseplates with surviving plank revetment jointed to the upright piles (Figure 40). This would appear to be a sluice structure, to control flow over the weir, but was equally effective funnelling the flow, presumably to catch fish and/or eels. Upstream of the V the river bed had been artificially raised and protected with alternate layers of wattle panels and gravel, all capped by a surface of stone blocks. Large oak baseplates were incorporated into this raised platform. Another large baseplate lay against the upstream side of the weir, just a few metres away from the platform, and possibly derived from it.

The baseplates displayed complex jointing suggesting they had once supported a plank floor. A series of dowel holes may also have indicated the former presence of a wooden grill. These features bear some resemblance to baseplates used in the Anglo-Saxon mill house and mill pool at Tamworth (Rahtz 1992) and the medieval timber head race at the Bordesley mill (Astill 1993). Together with the evidence suggested by a number of millstone roughouts located amongst the weir stones it would seem that a mill house once stood on or very near the weir and the massive timbers were re-used from that structure.

Construction of Weir

The weir was observed for 65m on a NE/SW alignment, diagonally crossing a Trent palaeochannel. Between the rows of posts it was *c.* 2.5m wide. Towards the southern end of the weir lay an area of raised Holme Pierrepont sands which may have formed an island *c.* 15m wide by at least 20m in length. The double row of posts continued for a further 8m to the south of the 'island', but with no further stones, which suggests it was possibly an open channel, crossed by a causeway raised on pile posts. The south bank of the channel was not located and was presumably removed as the river migrated southwards. The northern extent of the weir and the north bank of the river was obscured by a wide embankment separating the active quarry from the modern Trent.

Pile Posts

Sixty-one pile posts were observed in the construction of the double row of posts which supported the sides of the weir, recorded as an upstream (26 timbers) and a downstream alignment (35 timbers). Each alignment contained both large posts (*c.* 0.2–0.4m diameter) and small posts (*c.* 0.1–0.15m diameter). The larger posts were generally set some 0.4m downstream of the smaller posts and appeared to be driven more deeply into the underlying substrate (Figure 41 and Figure 42). While it could be assumed that one set of posts replaced the other there was no significant difference in the dates of the posts (discussed below, Figure 77) with complete felling dates from both large and small posts, upstream and downstream alignments all suggesting the timbers were felled between AD 1116–1120.

Twelve large posts were recorded from the upstream row, and 12 downstream; all were oak. Nineteen were recorded as whole timbers, three were squared whole timbers and two were unrecorded.

Thirty-seven posts (with diameters of less than 150mm) were recorded as the smaller rows of post alignments: 23 upstream and 14 downstream. Twenty-six were whole timbers, one squared whole, two quartered and eight unrecorded. Sixteen posts were recorded as oak, 16 'not oak' (two were subsequently identified as beech (C.R. Salisbury pers. comm.) and five unrecorded.

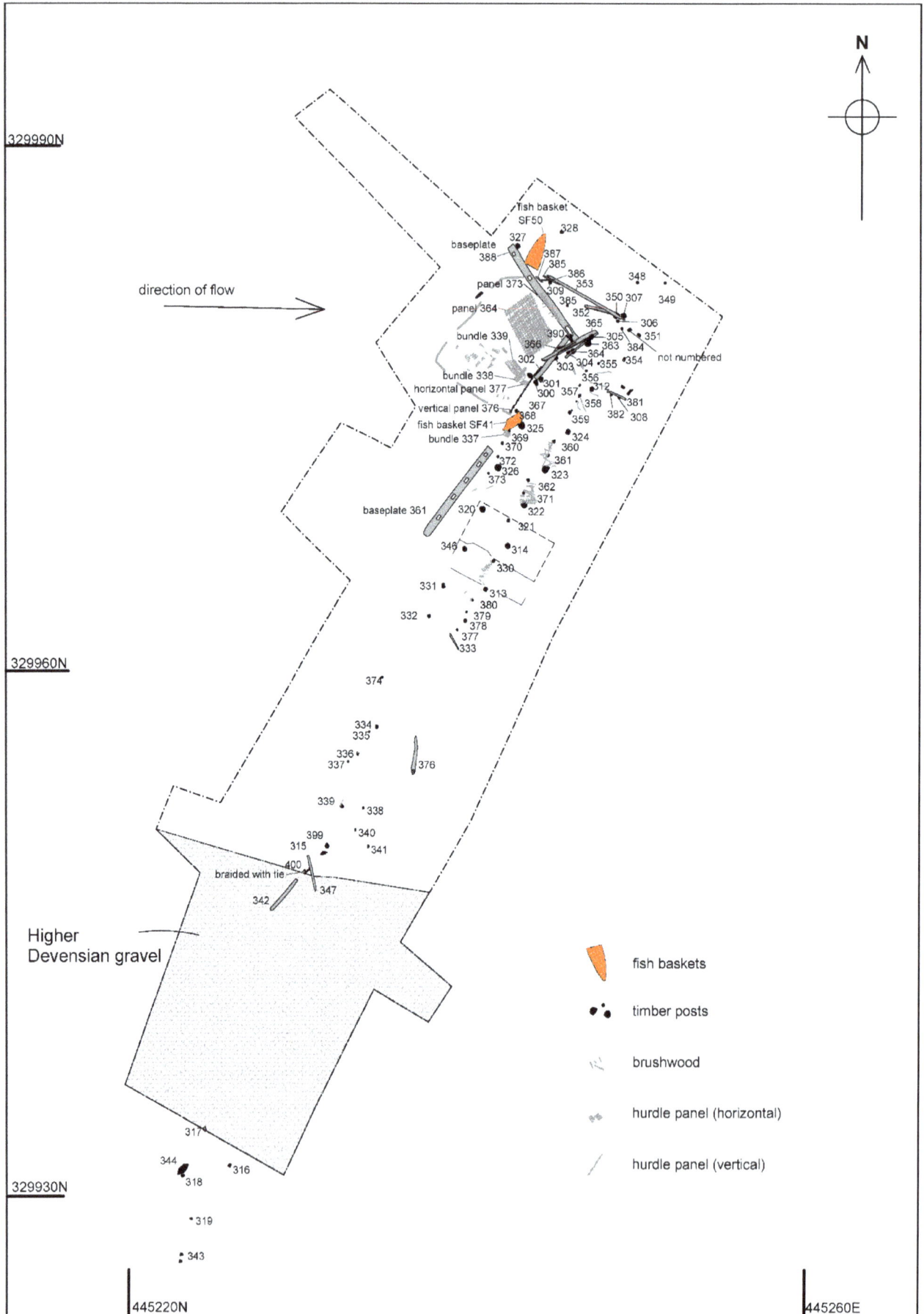

Figure 38: Plan of HL12 weir timbers including mill baseplates and hurdle panels.

N

unexcavated bund separating
quarry from modern Trent

329990N

anaerobic clay/silt

direction of flow

329960N

Transect 1:
Millstone Grit: 171 stones/71.36Kgs
Sandstone: 42 stones/18.77Kgs
Total: 213 stones/ 90.13Kgs
(X20 = c.2 Imperial tons of stone
used to fill the whole weir)

Ashlar blocks

Millstone Grit
(coarse unsorted sandstone)

Bromsgrove sandstone
(fine, soft, banded & sorted)

Other unidentified sandstone
(similar to Bromsgrove but purplish in colour)

Fish basket

Timber posts

Brushwood

Hurdle panel (horizontal)

Hurdle panel (vertical)

an island of high
Devensian sands

329930N

445220N

445260E

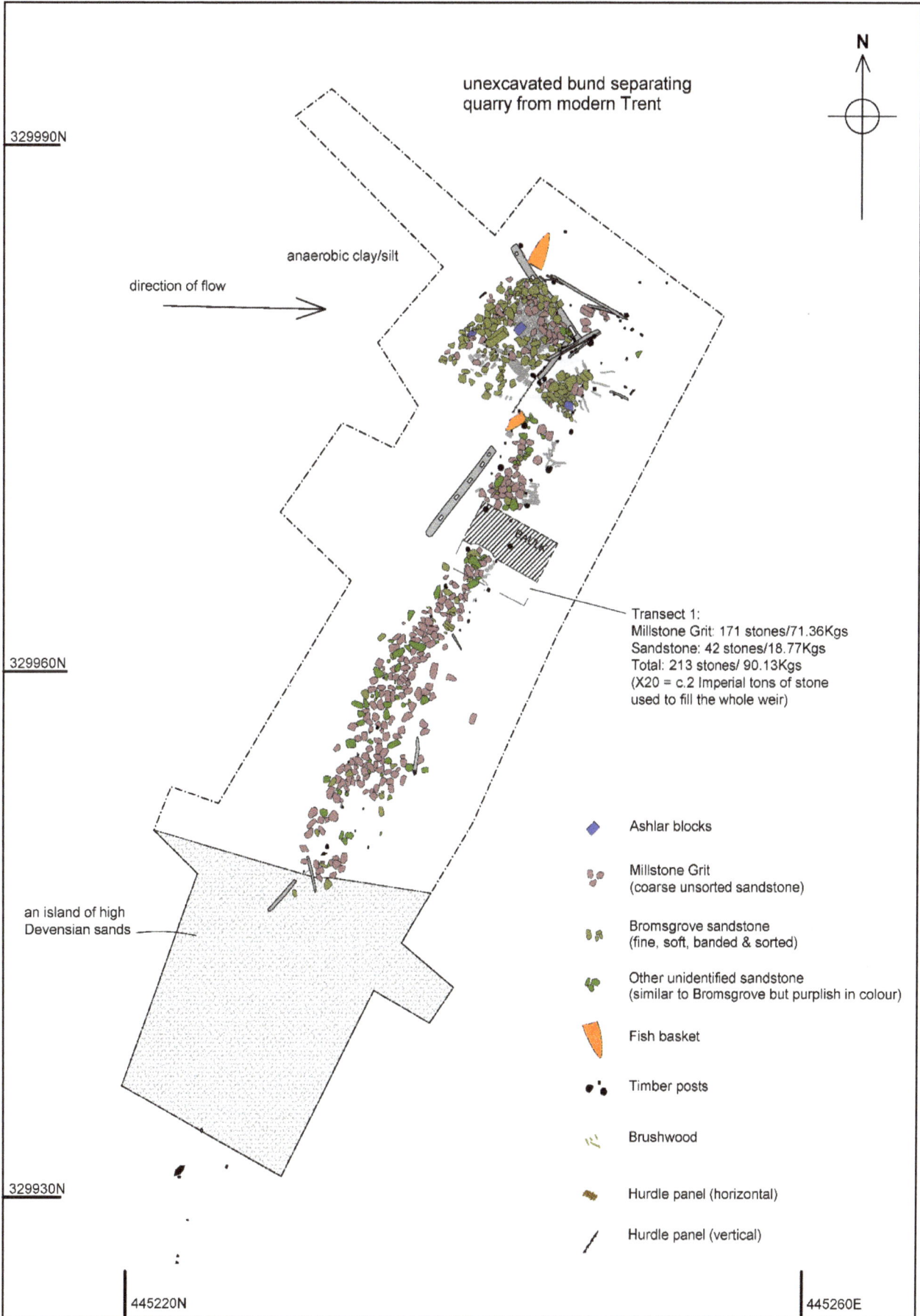

Figure 39: Plan of HL12 weir timbers including stone infill.

Figure 40: The HL12 weir, looking south showing upright posts (loosely 'marked' by the excavators) enclosing a rubble stone infill. The plank-lined V is in the foreground with the artificially raised platform of hurdle panels capped by stones to the right. The partially excavated wicker eel trap (SF50) is bottom right.

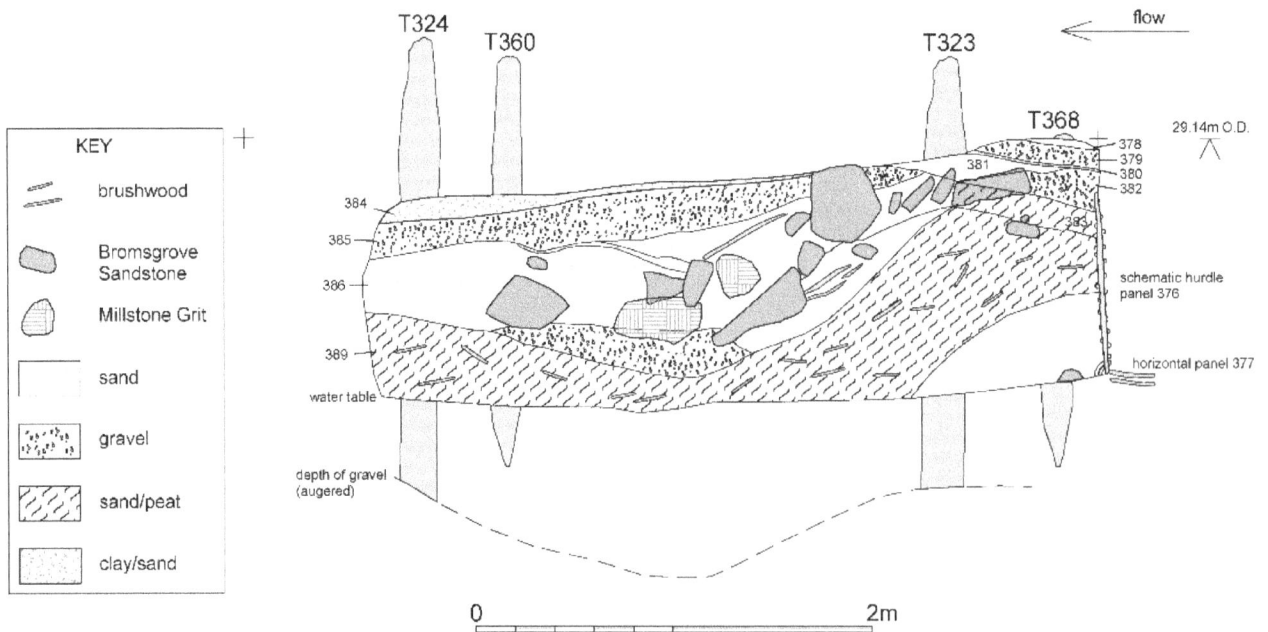

Figure 41: Transect 1 (located on Fig. 39) across weir. Note vertical Panel 376 and horizontal Panel 377 to the right.

Brushwood and Hurdle Crib

Within the two rows of posts the riverbed was lined with loose brushwood bundles, to prevent scouring (Figure 41 and Figure 42). The hand excavation of a transect across a well-preserved portion of the weir (Transect 1, Figure 39), revealed that the brushwood, although slightly haphazardly, was placed in alternate layers at 90° to each other. The bundles did not appear to be tied and were made up of a variety of twigs and branches (Figure 41). At the northern end of the weir, towards the deeper part of the river, the brushwood was noticeably thicker, while upstream of the weir, where scouring would have been most intense, prefabricated woven hurdle panels were laid

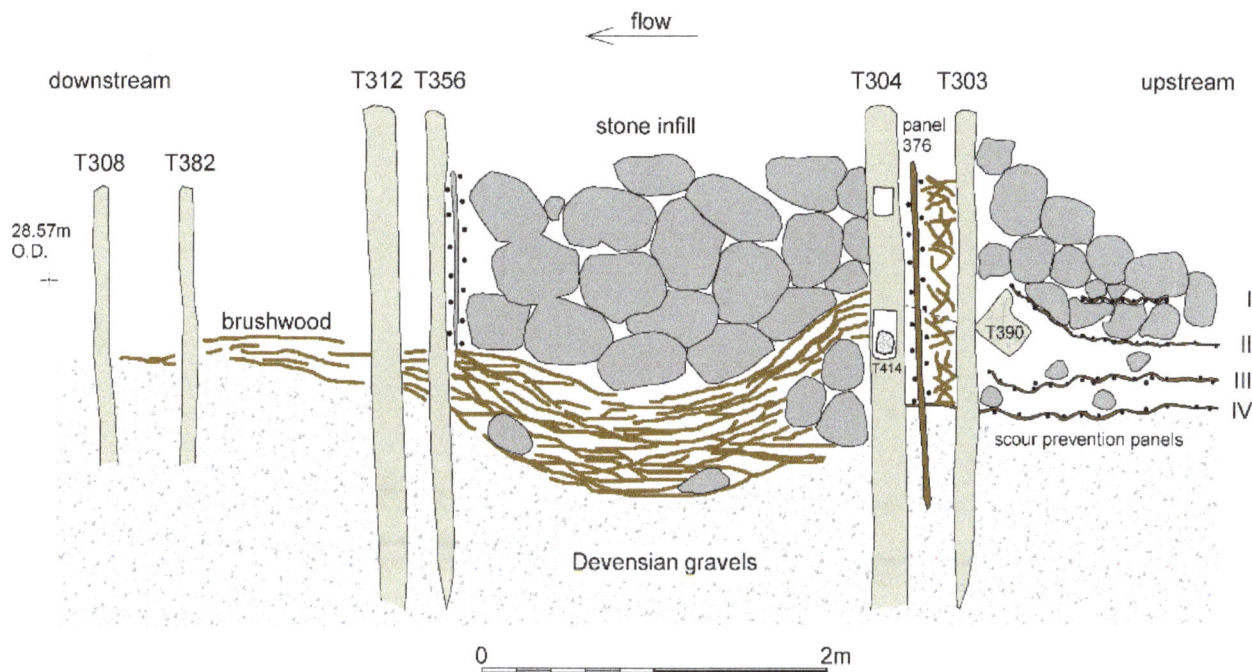

Figure 42: Sketch cross-section through the northern end of the weir including thick layers of brushwood bundles and the upstream scour prevention measures (Panels I – IV, stone blocks and Baseplate 390).

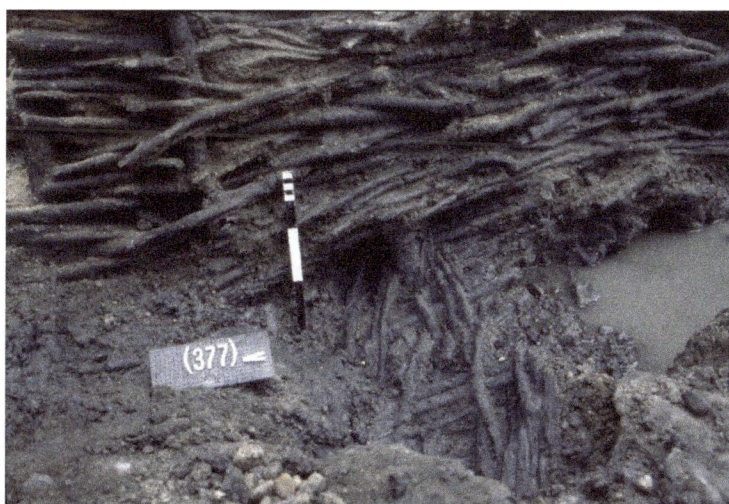

Figure 43: The Horizontal Panel 377 lying below the upright Panel 376.

on the riverbed (e.g. Panel 377 in Figure 41, Figure 43 and Figure 56).

The side walls of the weir were formed by vertical woven panels. Most of the hurdle panels were poorly preserved and had either collapsed in antiquity or were too fragile to excavate fully (e.g. Figure 44). The full length or height of each panel could not be discerned, no mechanism for attaching the panels to the uprights was seen, and it was not even generally possible to be sure which posts were intended to support which panels. One panel however, was well preserved: Panel 376 was robustly built with unusually large oak uprights (Figure 45). It measured 3m wide and survived to a height of 1.4m. It was made with nine upright posts or 'sails' (of which two were pairs of posts) bound with *c.* 30 rows of hazel rods. Often the rods were also

paired, but not ubiquitously so. No mechanism for binding the panel to the upright posts of the weir was observed and it remains uncertain whether the binding had broken/rotted away, or that they never existed and the panels were held to the posts by the flow of the river and perhaps stones around their bases. The unusually good preservation of Panel 376 suggests it may have been a replacement and it is clearly added after the horizontal Panel 377 was in place (see Figure 42).

Stone Infill

Once the crib of posts, brushwood base and hurdle walls, had been constructed, the weir was then filled with large stone blocks. The stones were of mixed sizes and types and there was no discernible pattern of distribution. Across

Figure 44: The less well-preserved vertical panel on the downstream face of the weir, between Posts 313 (left) and 330 (right).

Figure 45: The most complete vertical Panel 376 on the upstream face of the weir, towards the northern end of the weir. The unusually good preservation suggests it was a later, stronger addition to the weir.

the hand-excavated transect (Figure 39), the retrieved stones weighed 71.2 kg of Millstone Grit and 18.7 kg of sandstone. The transect comprised roughly 5% of the weir so it can be calculated that a minimum of 1,824 kg of stone must have been used on the weir. However, it should be noted that considerably more stones were used towards the deeper (northern) end of the weir and the real total was likely to have been well in excess of 2 metric tonnes.

A sample of Millstone Grit (Sample 108) and one of sandstone (Sample 109) were identified by Dr. R Clements (Geology, University of Leicester) as follows:

Sample 108: Millstone Grit (M. Carboniferous). Very coarse sandstone granules with lots of feldspar. Arkose rock type (a sandstone). Lower in the succession than the other sandstones. Could be from the Melbourne area (c. 8km upstream, just beyond King's Mill, Castle Donington).

Sample 109: Fine to medium grained sandstone with small amount of feldspar. Could be Triassic but more likely carboniferous. Probably from the Coal Measures.

V-Shaped Funnel

At the northern extent of the weir the upstream row of posts (Figure 38; Figures 46-53) changed trajectory and diagonally joined the southern row, thereby forming the southern arm of a V arrangement of timbers funnelling the river flow to a gap some 1.6m wide (between Posts 305 and 350, Figure 46). The V was asymmetric with the northern arm probably parallel to the northern bank, although the distance away from the river edge was not known. The apex of the V was at an angle of c. 59°.

The southern arm of the V was made up of an alignment of seven posts (Timbers 300, 301, 303, 304, 364, 363 and 305). Two of the posts (T304 and T305) had two sets of through mortices, an 'upper' and a 'lower' set, with a beam (T414) running through the lower set (Figure 47, Figure 48 and Figure 49). Beam 414 was circular in cross-section, 1.56m long (one end was broken in antiquity) by 140mm diameter: an unconverted oak branch. The northern end was 180mm higher than the southern end (28.42 and 28.24m AOD respectively), but was affected by a 'collapse

Figure 46: General view of the V-shaped funnel, looking south. The northern arm of the V lies across the bottom of the picture, note the partially excavated eel basket to the right. The southern arm has Plank 365 resting in front of it.

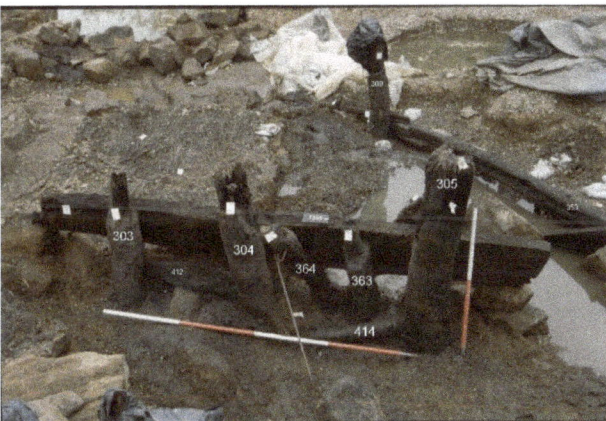

Figure 47: The downstream view (looking north-west) of the southern arm of the V, with the northern arm in the background.

tilt' in Post 304: it was probably constructed to be level. A surviving beam in the northern arm of the V (Beam 353) had a level upper surface at 28.46m AOD.

The cross-section of the beam only occupied half of the vertical length of both mortice holes (280mm long by 140mm wide, Figure 42, Post 304/Beam 414), suggesting the likelihood that another beam may also have run through the hole, forming a continuation. If a beam in the upper set of mortices were projected northwards it would meet T350, one of the uprights supporting the beam of the northern arm of the V, which includes two dowel holes on its corresponding east face, at the same height (c. 29.03 and 29.20m AOD, Figure 52). The use of dowel pegs as a fixing would suggest the beam was not a detachable barrier, but was intended to be permanent. The beam may have been fixed apparatus associated with supporting either fish baskets or nets.

The upper mortice holes in Posts 304 and 305 appeared to be of a similar width to the lower mortices, but were shorter

Figure 48: Tenoned Post 303 with through mortice in Post 304 (upper pair) behind, both from the southern arm of the V. Note the end of Baseplate 390 to the right.

(c. 160mm), perhaps designed to accommodate only one beam (Figure 48). Timber Posts 363 and 303, from the same alignment of posts, both had tenons cut into their tops

Figure 49: Post 305 (nearest), Beam 414 and Post 304, southern arm of the V. Note the upper and lower (larger) courses of through mortices.

(Figure 48). Although both posts were slightly tilting, it is conceivable that the tenons once aligned with the through mortices, to provide a 'belt-and-braces' method of securing the uppermost horizontal element of the structure.

Wedged up against Posts 303 and 304, behind Post 364 and above Beam 414 lay another horizontal timber, T412 (Figure 49). T412 was a plank 1.28m long by 190mm wide by 70mm thick. It was cut to a point at one end and had a series of joints that could not have been used as the timber was found. Timber 412 was clearly re-used and will be discussed more fully below.

On the upstream side of all the posts grouped as the southern arm of the V, but clearly later even than the stone scour prevention platform (discussed below) was a very large oak plank (T365). Timber 365 was resting on its side, but tilting and sloping down from south down to the north by 340mm. It was not jointed to any of the posts but the broad face of the plank included pairs of dowel holes towards either end of the plank (Figures 46 and 58), one pair re-drilled, and two further dowel pegs on the upper edge of the plank. The dowel peg holes were between 28–38mm wide and wooden tree-nails were still present in four of the eight holes. No corresponding holes were found on the upright pile posts, although holes that distance apart were noted on Post 350 (northern arm of V). The plank may have been part of the V structure, or it may simply have washed in and come to rest against the southern arm of the V.

The northern arm of the V consisted of five large pile posts (Timbers 327, 309, 350, 306 and 307) and a possible further two (351 and 384) extending downstream (located on Figure 38). Passing through a mortice in the Pile Post 350 was rectangular Beam 353 (5.18m long by160 x 150mm cross-section, upper face at 28.46m AOD). Beam 353 was prevented from pulling out of the through mortice in T350 in two ways: a slight shoulder cut into the beam (Figures 50 and 52) thereby forming a tenon and a through dowel peg preventing the tenon from coming out of the mortice,

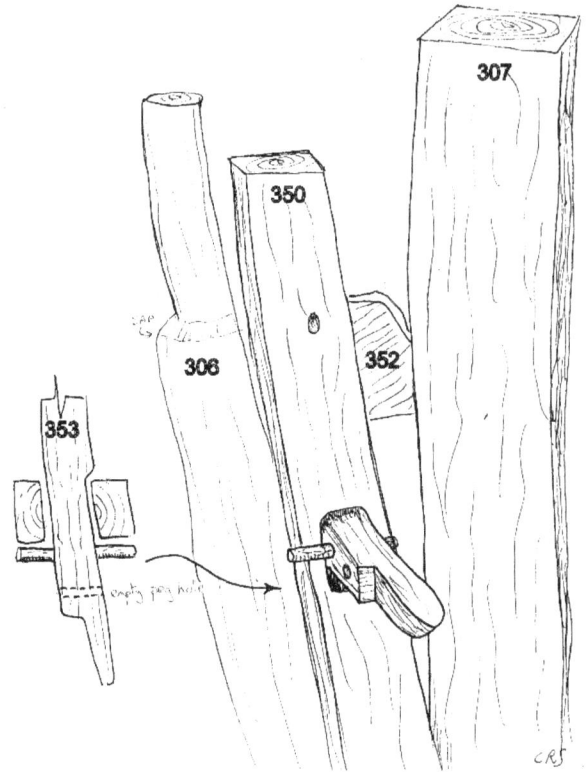

Figure 50: Sketch looking NW, of pegged joint.

in the manner of 'tusk tenon'. The very tip of Beam 353 was also cut as a tenon/end lap that would presumably have connected it to another beam, although dowel pegs to secure this joint were notably absent. The end of Beam 353 was prevented from moving either northwards or southwards by Pile Posts 307 and 306 respectively, which 'pegged' the beam in position. The tops of Posts 307 and 350 were both cross-cut flat, suggesting that they survived to their full height (29.52 and 29.32m AOD), and were not jointed to a superstructure.

The north-west end of Beam 353, had also been cut to a tenon (Figure 51), but in this instance a through dowel suggests how the joint was fastened to another timber. Indeed, the similar dimensions on a tenon on the end of Beam 385 (found wedged behind Beam 353), suggest it could easily have been the continuation of Beam 353. It was 1.12m long but broken at its northern end. The north-west end of Beam 353 did not appear to rest in a mortice hole; either the pile post with mortice was removed during the collapse of the structure, or the beam was only attached to a pile post by means of a dowel peg. Post 309 would have prevented the Beam 353 from moving in a southerly direction, in the manner of Post 307 at the other end (Figure 38), but no post restricting movement to the north survived.

Pile Post 309 also included a through mortice at a higher level. The top of the mortice was at 29.10m AOD, the same height as that recorded for the top of the upper through mortice recorded on Post 305 from the southern arm of the V. The mortice in Post 309 would have supported a beam on a northeast/southwest alignment: at right angles to Beam 353. On the southeast face of Post 350 two dowel

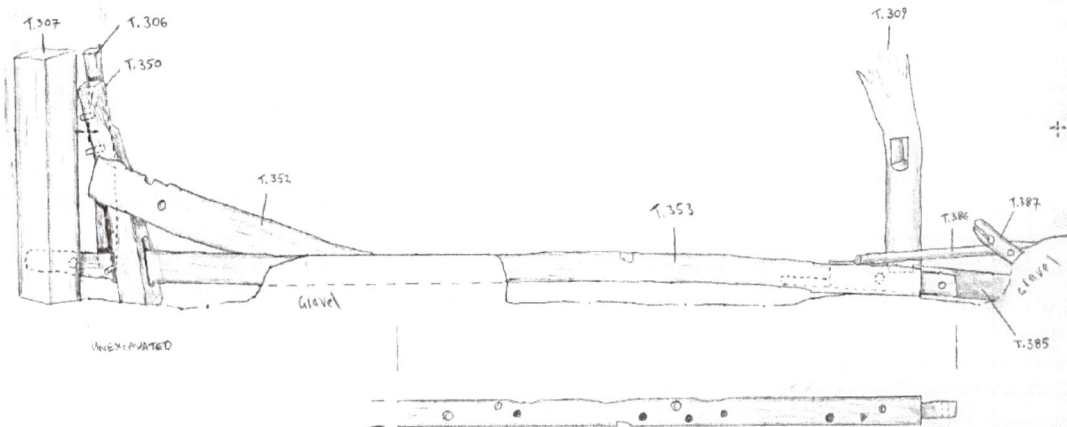

Figure 51: Measured section of the downstream side of the north arm of the V (looking south). At the bottom of the picture is a sketch of the upper face of Beam 353 with numerous dowel holes.

Figure 52: The peg securing of Beam 353 to Post 350, northern arm of the V. Note the tops of Posts 350 (centre) and 307 (right) were both cut flat in antiquity, suggesting they were not jointed to a superstructure.

pegs were noted. At 200mm apart (at 29.02 and 29.22m AOD) it is conceivable that the pegs mark the point at which the upper beam of the southern arm of the V met the northern arm forming the apex of the V.

The upper face of Beam 353 was level at 28.46m AOD, the same height as the lower beam (414) on the southern arm. Only part of the beam was fully excavated but over a 3m stretch (see Figure 51) 10 dowel pegs were noted. The pegs were all had *c.* 35mm diameter holes, six wooden pegs were found *in situ* and the holes appeared to be slightly clustered in groups of three or four. The gaps between the

groups were *c.* 550mm wide. The function of the dowel holes was not clear but the pegs in these holes may once have supported a plank flooring, or upright pegs may have acted as a grille or they may even have been a mechanism for securing fish baskets in the flow of the river.

Lying above Beam 353 at an extremely tilted angle was Plank 352 (Figure 51). The plank was 230mm wide by 40mm thick and traced for 2m (it was then too far below the water table to be pursued). Two dowel holes were observed at one end of the plank, but it was not clear which posts the plank had originally been jointed to.

It was not possible to excavate even an exploratory trench to the south (downstream) of the V due the the level of the water table and rapid ingress of water. A dark silt area suggests the riverbed had been considerably deeper, presumably the result of scouring.

Scour Prevention Platform

Immediately upstream of the V the river bed was clearly vulnerable to erosion. The earliest surviving method of defence to counter this took the form of massive baseplate timbers being used to deflect the flow (Figure 38). Baseplate 390 was placed horizontally on the gravel riverbed at the base of Pile Posts 301 and 303, aligned with the upstream row of posts that formed the weir (Figure 53). A second baseplate (T361) was placed on a similar alignment but 4.75m south of T390. Baseplate 361 had shifted from its original position (the northern end was 1.5m higher than the south, Figure 54), but may have originally been placed at the base of Posts 346, 320 and 326. A third baseplate, T388, lay at 90° to the north end of Baseplate 390. T388 was 'pegged' to the riverbed at its eastern end, with pile Post 389 passing through a double through mortice hole (Figure 55). Both timbers were below the natural water-table and it was only possible to even glimpse these timbers with the support of a number of water-pumps.

The three massive baseplates (361, 388 and 390) were clearly re-used timbers; all had numerous large through mortices with no corresponding tenons, numerous unused dowel holes and Baseplate 388 had a half-lap on the underside face. The Pile Post 389 'pegging' the end of Baseplate 388 (Figure 53) was clearly small and round in cross-section and did not fit the large rectangular through mortice. The jointing demonstrated on the baseplates and the possible origins of these timbers are discussed further below.

Figure 53: The archaeologist is sitting on Baseplate 388 which tilts into a scour hole at the apex of the V. The higher Baseplate 390 is at the height of the original river bed.

Within the 'L' formed by Baseplates 388 and 390, was a series of at least four layers of horizontal hurdle panels hurdle panel (Panels I-IV, Figure 42). The earliest Panel IV was placed on the gravel riverbed, but overlapped the baseplates (Figure 56, middle). It was only partially exposed, but was 3.5m long (height unknown) and made up of *c.* 12 sails/uprights (either single timbers or in groups of two), with plainly woven single rods/horizontals. Each of the subsequent panels was separated by layers of dark grey silty sand with occasional large sandstone blocks, placed to 'anchor' the panels. Full excavation of all the hurdle panels was not possible, but the uppermost panel (Panel I, Figure 56, right) was fully exposed.

Panel I (context 364) was near complete, 3.5m long by 2.3m high, but neither twisted over ends nor clearly cut sail ends were observed, so the panel may have been larger. The sails appeared to taper towards the centre of the panel, although none could be followed to its complete length. The 16 sails were generally in groups of two-three, approximately 20mm thick and up to 30mm at the base. Rods were plainly woven. The rods were around 15–20mm diameter and mainly woven in groups of two, usually parallel, but some twisted together. Single rods appeared to have been deliberately woven at an angle and this seems to be restricted to the central portion of the panel. The angled rods may have served as a method of bracing.

Panel I was weighed down with numerous large stones (Figure 39, Figure 40 and Figure 46). The area covered by the stones encompassed *c.* 35m² and was rectangular in plan, 7m long (north-east to south-west) by 5m wide (north-west to south-east) although it was not clear how much of the platform was formally laid-out with hurdles. Towards the upstream edge of the platform, although brushwood was plentiful, it was difficult to differentiate broken-up panels from brushwood bundles.

The Timber Used in HL12

Five timbers within the weir can be interpreted as re-used elements as they were clearly cut to serve a function that was not evident in the weir as it was found.

Figure 54: Left, Baseplate 361, not in its original location, but on a similar alignment to Baseplate 390. Right, detail of Baseplate 361 showing large through mortices, numerous dowel holes in a recessed area (perhaps originally to support a plank floor) and a baton, doweled into the recess, on opposite side.

Figure 55: The lower end of Baseplate 388 with two squared mortice holes. Note the smaller round Pile Post 389 apparently pegging the baseplate to the riverbed. Post 389 has not been cut to fit the corresponding mortice and suggests 388 was a later addition.

Figure 56: Three views of the scour prevention platform. Left: Baseplate 388 with Baseplate 390 in the distance at 90° to T388 and at a higher level. T390 lies on the gravel river bed while 388 tilts into a scour towards the apex of the V. Middle: the lowest hurdle panel (Panel IV) lapping over both baseplates with Panel I above. Right: The uppermost Panel I following the removal of the top layer of stones (see Figure 42 and Figure 46).

Baseplate 361 (Figure 54 and Figure 57) was found parallel, but a short distance upstream of the stone weir, dislodged and tilting. The south end was 1.5m lower than the north, and beneath the water table: it could only be recorded by touch. It was probable that the southern end was broken.

This massive timber was converted to a boxed heart trunk (to retain its bulk), at least 6m long by 0.5m wide by 0.32m thick. The surface of the timber was extremely water worn

and no tool marks were visible. Down the centre of the baseplate were five (of a probable six) through mortices (A-E, Figure 57). Assuming a sixth mortice had existed at the southern end, the baseplate would originally have had a pair of roughly square (0.2 x 0.15m), straight-sided through mortices at either end. A short distance in (0.35m), were a pair of larger angled through mortices (0.4 x 0.2m), projecting through-posts out towards the ends of the baseplate (see reconstruction 23), presumably to brace the uprights at each end and prevent lateral shearing. The

Baseplate 361

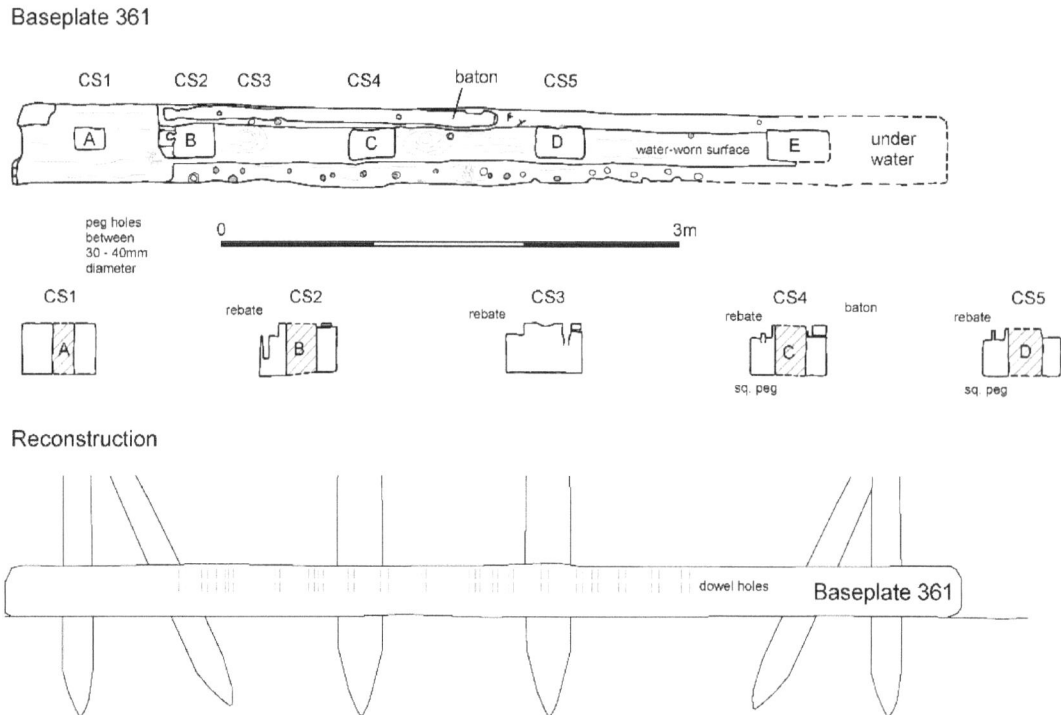

Figure 57: Baseplate 361 with possible reconstruction (below) suggested by a series of through mortices.

bracing lay within the length of the baseplate suggesting the superstructure encompassed the full length of the baseplate (6m). This differs from, for example, the baseplates with 'external' bracing observed on the Hemington Bridge structures (Ripper and Cooper, 2009, Figs. 25 and 55) where the bracing ran from the ends of the baseplate up to a superstructure that was narrower than the length of the baseplate. Baseplate 361 would have supported the side of a building at least 6m long.

Towards the centre of Baseplate 361 a third pair of through mortices (C and D, Figure 57) indicate another pair of uprights ran through the baseplate, with a central gap 0.93m wide. The central through mortices were larger than the end mortices, suggesting they supported a greater structural weight. The corners of both mortices were drilled, leaving a distinct rounded profile. A tight-fitting squared joint was obviously not needed; the stability of the structure relied on weight and perhaps an earthfast element. The distance (centre to centre) between the small, square mortice A and the larger, rectangular C was 1.80m, similar to the distance between comparable mortices on Baseplate 388 (see below in this section).

As all the mortices were through-mortices it suggests that either the baseplate was jointed to other timbers or that the uprights projected into the ground below in the 'earthfast' tradition. The similarity of these timbers and their joints to those observed in the earliest Hemington Bridge (Darrah 2009a, 100–113), and particularly because the joints appear to not have been tight fitting, suggests that the latter 'earthfast' interpretation is the more probable.

Along both edges of the upper face of the baseplate a longitudinal recess was cut. The recesses did not extend over the full length of the timber; it was inset by 1m at the northern end, and was likely to be symmetrical at the south. Along the western edge (the lower edge as illustrated in Figure 57) the recess was up to 0.16m wide by 0.08m deep and included at least 20 dowel holes. It is suggested that the dowels once pegged the ends of plank flooring, running perpendicular to the baseplate. The plethora of holes suggests the planking was replaced on at least one occasion.

The recess along the eastern edge (upper edge as illustrated in Figure 57) included an attached baton, pegged at either end. The baton was also oak, 2.2m long by 100 x 60mm cross-section, pegged with two split heartwood oak pegs. Along the back edge of the recess was a narrow gap (30–50mm) between the baton and the baseplate, perhaps to 'sandwich' the base of upright planks or cladding. Two dowel pegs were also observed in the base of the gap.

Plank 365 (Figure 46, Figure 47 and Figure 58) was a tangentially split oak plank, 3.61m long by 480mm wide by 100mm thick. There were pairs of dowel holes at each end of the plank (*c.* 2.15m apart), but the pair at the southernmost end had been re-drilled. The dowel holes were 32 – 38mm in diameter, with a 220 – 250mm gap between the two holes in each pair (comparable to the spacing of the dowel holes seen on Post 350, part of the apex of the V). The monumental dimensions of the plank suggest it may be from the same structure as the baseplates but it was not jointed to other timbers and was found resting above the hurdle and stone scour prevention platform.

Baseplate 388 (Figure 55 and Figure 59) was located at the north end of the weir and formed the northern edge of the scour prevention platform. It had submerged into a deep

Plank 365

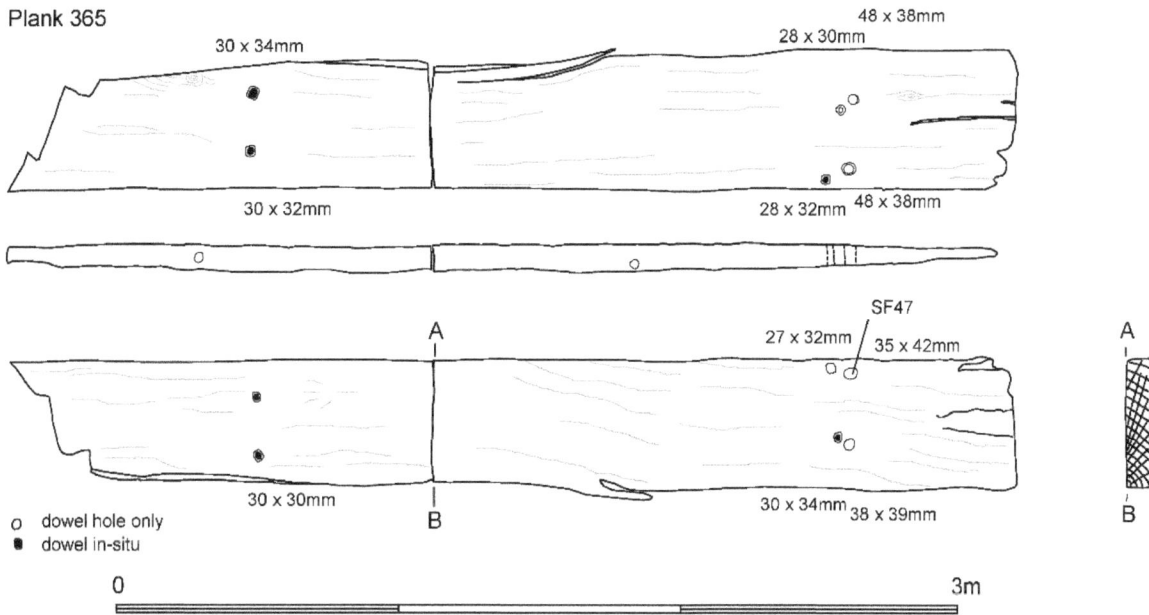

o   dowel hole only
●   dowel in-situ

Figure 58: Plank 365, with pairs of dowel pegs, one set re-drilled.

Timber 388

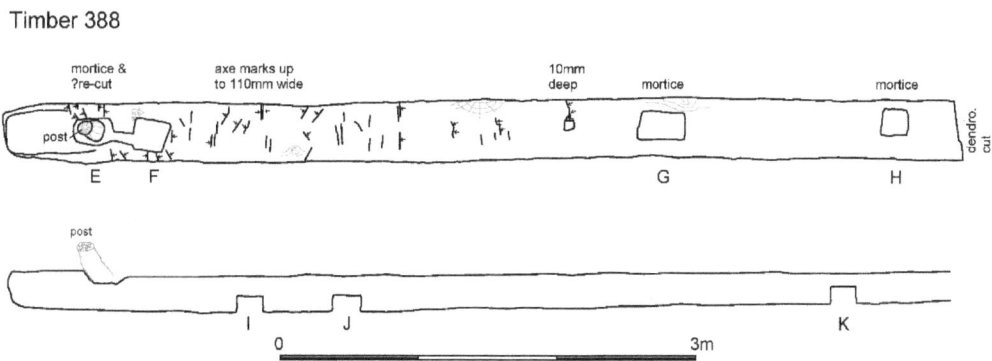

Figure 59: Baseplate 388, with through mortices (E, F, G and H) and half-lap jointing (I, J and K).

scour and its eastern end was below the water table, barely accessible.

The baseplate was oak, 6.95m long by 0.41 x 0.25m wide. The timber was cut square, but each surface was left rough with numerous tool marks. Weakening cuts across the surface of the baseplate indicates that the surface was hewn, not sawn. Tool profiles suggest the axe used was at least 110mm wide.

Four through mortices were recorded on the upper face of Timber 388: E was 0.28 x 0.20m, F 0.24 x 0.22m, G 0.35 x 0.20m and H 0.20 x 0.20m. E and G were rectangular, F and H square. E and F were immediately adjacent to each other, and a segment of the wood between them had split away, joining the two holes.

The distance between the pairs (centre to centre) was E – G = 4.10m, F – H = 5.40m. The distance between G and H, (the large rectangular mortice and the smaller square mortice, centre to centre) was 1.75m, the same distance as that between comparable mortices on Baseplate 361 (rectangular C and square A, Figure 57). These

combinations of through mortices of different sizes at similar distances apart provide the strongest indication that the timbers derived from the same structure.

On the opposing side of Baseplate 388 three half-lap joints were indentified (E, F and G, Figure 59). It was not possible to turn the timber, so the joints were only recorded from the side elevation. Two of the half-laps were close enough to suggest one may have replaced the other (E and F had only a 0.5m gap between them). The timber was not in the location for which the laps were cut: they lay face down on the gravel riverbed.

Baseplate 390 was placed horizontally on the gravel riverbed at the base of Pile Posts 301 and 303, aligned with the upstream weir posts. In plan it was perpendicular to Baseplate 388 forming an 'L' shaped edge to the scour prevention platform, but the two baseplates were not joined (Figure 38 and Figure 53).

Baseplate 390 was a squared oak timber. The water-worn surface precluded the survival of tool marks. It was over 3m long (0.30 x 0.30m wide) but the southern extreme was broken and worn in antiquity. A longitudinal recess was cut out of the full length of the timber, 80mm deep, 180mm wide, with the back of the recess water-worn. Towards the northern end a pair of through mortices was cut (0.11 x 0.08m and 0.13 x 0.08m). These mortices were 0.68m from the end of the timber but only 0.10m apart from each other: one may have replaced the other. Some 2.8m from the end of the baseplate a third through mortice was observed (0.24 x 0.08m). All three mortices were cut through the whole timber, not the recess. No dowel holes were observed in the recess, although it should be noted that the timber was only uncovered on the last day of excavation, and hurriedly recorded.

Timber 412 (Figure 60) was found horizontal, but wedged into the posts associated with the southern arm of the V. One end was cut to a point, the other cut square. Along one edge of the timber a recess had been cut (60mm wide by 20mm deep) which suggests the timber was once edge-lapped to another timber. Half-way along the timber, on the opposite edge, an edge through mortice (?half lap) was cut (180mm wide). Four dowel holes were identified (*c.* 35mm diameter) through the face of the plank, two with wooden dowel pegs *in situ*. The original function of these jointing mechanisms was not clear but seemed to suggest 412 was a 'corner post', supporting timbers going in two different directions (Figure 60).

Timber 412

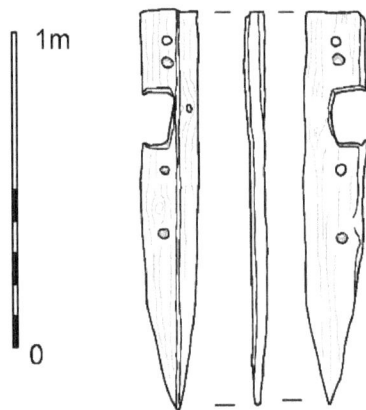

sketch reconstruction

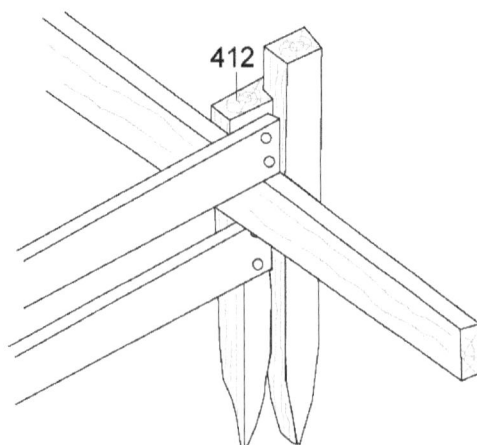

Figure 60: Post 412, with conjectural reconstruction of post jointing.

Discussion of the Timbers

Four of the timbers (T361, 365, 388 and 390) were of monumental proportions and displayed a series of joints, suggesting they originated from a jointed structure. Through mortices for uprights and bracings, half-lap joints and dowel pegs were numerous but served no function in the positions in which the timbers were found. The half-laps on Baseplate 388 were face-down on the gravels, and must once have been jointed to another timber. While the function of the original structure is not known nor indeed that they originated from a single structure, there is circumstantial evidence to suggest both.

All four timbers appeared to have been prepared from similarly large oak trunks hewn in a similar way with little effort made to remove weakening cuts to produce a flat surface. It may have been that flat surfaces were not felt to be necessary for the accurate joining of timbers (see 'Hewing timbers to shape' Darrah 2009b, 132–4) or that the structure was not intended to be visible (?underwater). Tool signatures were not identifiable.

Although recording wear-patterns on water-logged timbers is inevitably a subjective exercise, it is worth noting the excavators' impressions of the timbers. Two of the baseplates (T361 and 390) were very water-worn, Baseplate 388 less so despite its location at the apex of the V. Baseplate 361 was mostly worn along the length of the timber, the cross-sections, particularly over the recesses, appeared to have remained square. Timber 390, on the other hand, was more worn in cross-section. As both timbers were positioned against the weir on a similar alignment it is possible that the wear occurred during the original manifestation of the structure. This implies the original structure lay within the flow of the river.

The combination of small square mortices at the ends of baseplates coupled with larger rectangular through mortices *c.* 1.8m away is seen on both Baseplates 361 and 388. On Baseplate 390 the distance between the closest square and rectangular through mortices was slightly larger at 1.95m, but is of similar dimensions.

Long recesses were recorded on Baseplates 361 and 388; on Baseplate 390 the recess is 0.17m wide by 0.08m deep; on Baseplate 361 it is again 0.08m deep but the timber appears to have been worn completely away along one edge (see Figure 57 where dowel holes have been almost entirely removed where the edge has been lost). It is probable that the recesses supported either ends of horizontal planking.

The angled bracing seen on Baseplate 361 suggests the posts at the ends of the baseplate formed the ends of the structure; this suggests a structure around 6m long. The structure may have included plank flooring (between Baseplates 361 and 390). If the baseplate were held a set distance apart by the laps in Baseplate 388 the gap between the laps suggests a building either 4.11m or 3.40m wide. The laps did not have through mortices within them, so the efficacy of the joint would have depended on the weight of another timber/lap securing the two timbers together. It is unlikely that Baseplates 361 and 388 would have been pegged together with a post running through the through mortices as in both instances the mortice holes have their long edge parallel to the grain of the timber.

Although no direct equivalent for these timbers has been established, a near comparable set appears to be the remains of the second mill at Tamworth (Rahtz and Meeson 1992, 10 and 17–31) where a plank lined 'trough' controlled water running from the mill pond to the mill breast and wheel. The sill at the edge of the trough was of large squared baseplates, secured by large, horizontal through mortices. There are even indications that a horizontal wall was set in a groove (not unlike the 'groove' created by the baton, set into the recess on Baseplate 361). The planks, at Tamworth, were tight fitting within the sill but were neither set in a recess nor secured with dowels. There are no indications of internal bracing at Tamworth.

Perhaps a closer parallel can be suggested in the 12th century Mill Dam 500m downstream from HL12 (Figure 1). The timbers from Phase II (Clay and Salisbury 1990) show the use of monumental baseplates used to form a rectangular structure jointed by half-laps and secured with earthfast posts in through mortices (Figure 61). One of the baseplates included a recess with six dowel holes which may have secured a plank floor. The structure was interpreted to be a secondary dam, constructed perpendicular to the main dam and designed to create a head of water which could then be controlled through a sluice before entering a mill race. On HL12 a similar area of hard-standing perpendicular to the main weir structure was interpreted as a scour prevention platform. While this was undoubtedly its ultimate manifestation, the location of the vast baseplates beneath the layers of hurdle panels and stones, although no longer jointed, had perhaps not moved far from their original location. It is easy to envisage the baseplates originally formed part of a mill house structure. The main dam was constructed of timber pile posts, infilled with sandstone rubble, in much the same way as the HL12 weir but without the survival of the hurdle panelling. Some 15m downstream of the Hemington Fields Mill Dam the remains of part of a timber wheel breasting (for a vertical mill wheel) were found, as well as several broken millstones, confirming the presence of a water mill on the site (Clay and Salisbury 1990). While the timbers from HL12 were clearly not in their original location the similarities of the layout of the weir and the perpendicular 'secondary dam' is notable.

Fishing from the Weir

Eel Baskets

The remains of two wicker eel baskets were found in association with the HL12 weir. Basket SF50, a large, near perfectly-preserved trap was located immediately upstream of the northern arm of the V, 5m northwest of the apex, and the less well-preserved SF41 was located on top of the stone infill of the weir, adjacent to Post 325 (Figure 38). The mouth of SF50 was aligned with Beam 353 (i.e. the northern arm of the V, immediately over, but not apparently attached to Timber 385. The basket appeared to be held in place just by two small 'anchor stones', woven onto the basket. Assuming the basket was in its original location it would have been designed to catch silver eels on a downstream migration heading back to the sea.

Basket SF41 was very broken-up. As found the mouth lay between Posts 325 and 368 and was facing towards the north bank of the river. It was also secured by two small anchor stones

The baskets would have been inspected for catches; their open weave would have allowed for inspection without lifting. When eels were found the baskets would have been lifted and their bases opened by release of the handle and bung. They were probably poured into a sack.

Eel Basket SF50: the external plan view of eel basket SF50 was of a large openwork cone, over 2m long and 0.9m wide at the mouth tapering to 0.15m at its terminus (Figures 62–71). Careful dismantling revealed a tripartite, but inter-woven construction, thereby forming two internal funnels (non-return valves) leading to a catching chamber. It had a flat base and was semi-circular in cross-section at the mouth. A withy rope, integral to the basket, which also formed a handle, closed the terminus. A second withy rope handle was woven into the top of the entrance. The trap was weighted by two small waisted cobbles woven into the sides of the basket. This feature provides support to Mynard's (1979) speculation that pairs of waisted cobbles, some with withy traces, found by divers in the Thames were the remnants of fish baskets.

The basket was constructed as three baskets woven together to form the whole (Figure 62). First a small wide-mouthed cone was formed, 0.45m long by 0.80m wide (Basket I). It appeared to have been constructed on a D-shaped frame (the mouth) made from six year old hazel. One straight rod was used to form the flat base and two curved rods formed the curve of the D. Where the two rods met one rod was kinked to form a handle (Figure 69). Some 26 stakes were attached to the straight segment and around 50 to the curved part, giving a total of 76 stakes, each less than 20mm apart. The stakes were then made rigid and gradually drawn together by a series of seven rings woven to form hoops around the stakes. The hoops were attached as 'waling rods' (where a number of withies are worked through the stakes simultaneously to form a plaited pattern). For Basket I Type A '3 rod waling' (Figure 62) was used, where three pairs of rods were woven, two in-front, one behind. At the terminus Basket I was 160mm wide.

Once Basket I was completed Basket II was attached. *c.* 80 stakes, 1.4m long, that formed the ribs of the second basket were threaded into Basket I, passing through the third hoop

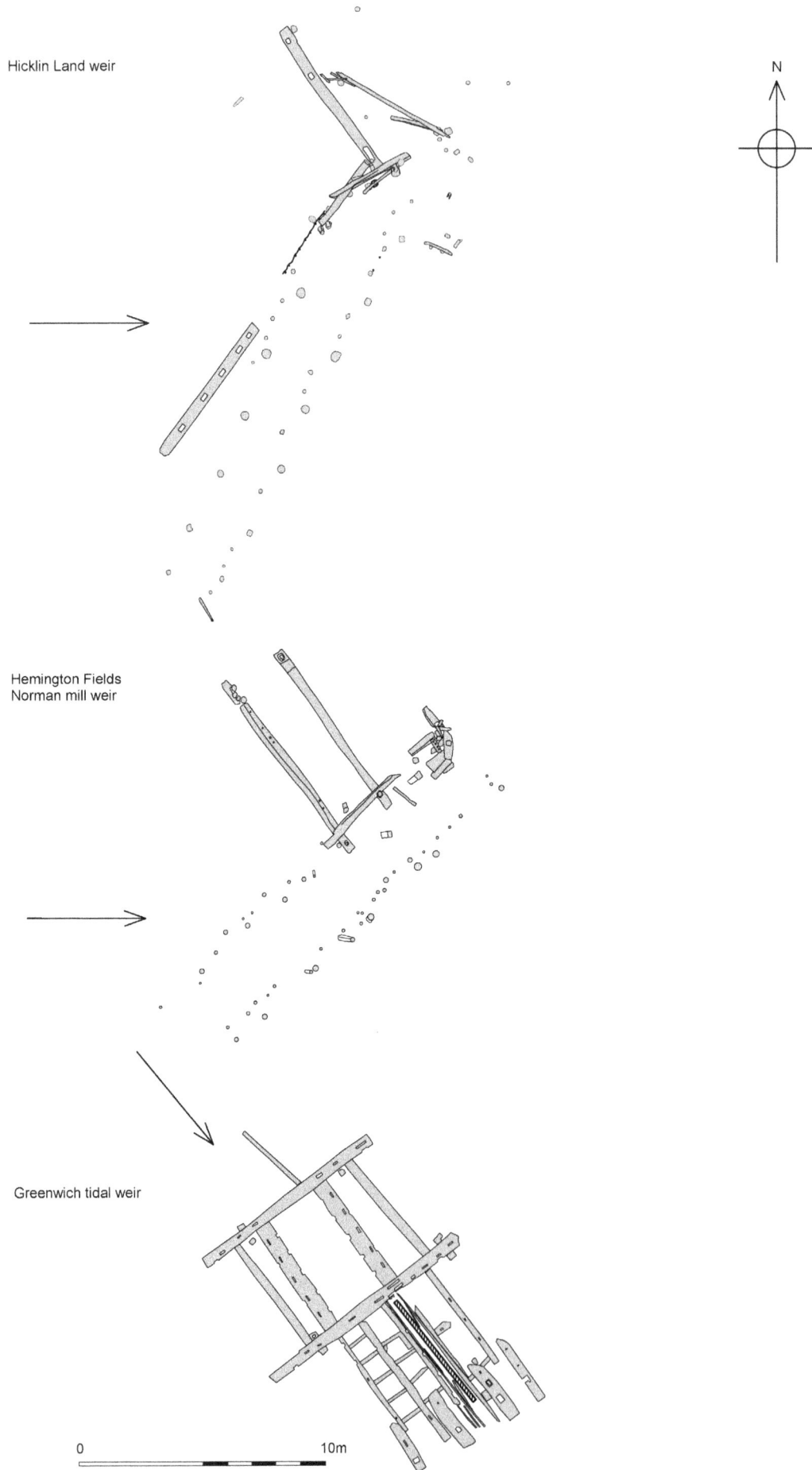

Hicklin Land weir

Hemington Fields
Norman mill weir

Greenwich tidal weir

0   10m

Figure 61: Comparison of recorded timber weirs: Top – Hemington Quarry (Hicklin Land) 2000, Middle – Pontylue Quarry (Hemington Fields) 1985 (Clay and Salisbury 1990) and Bottom – Greenwich Tidal Weir (Davis 2009).

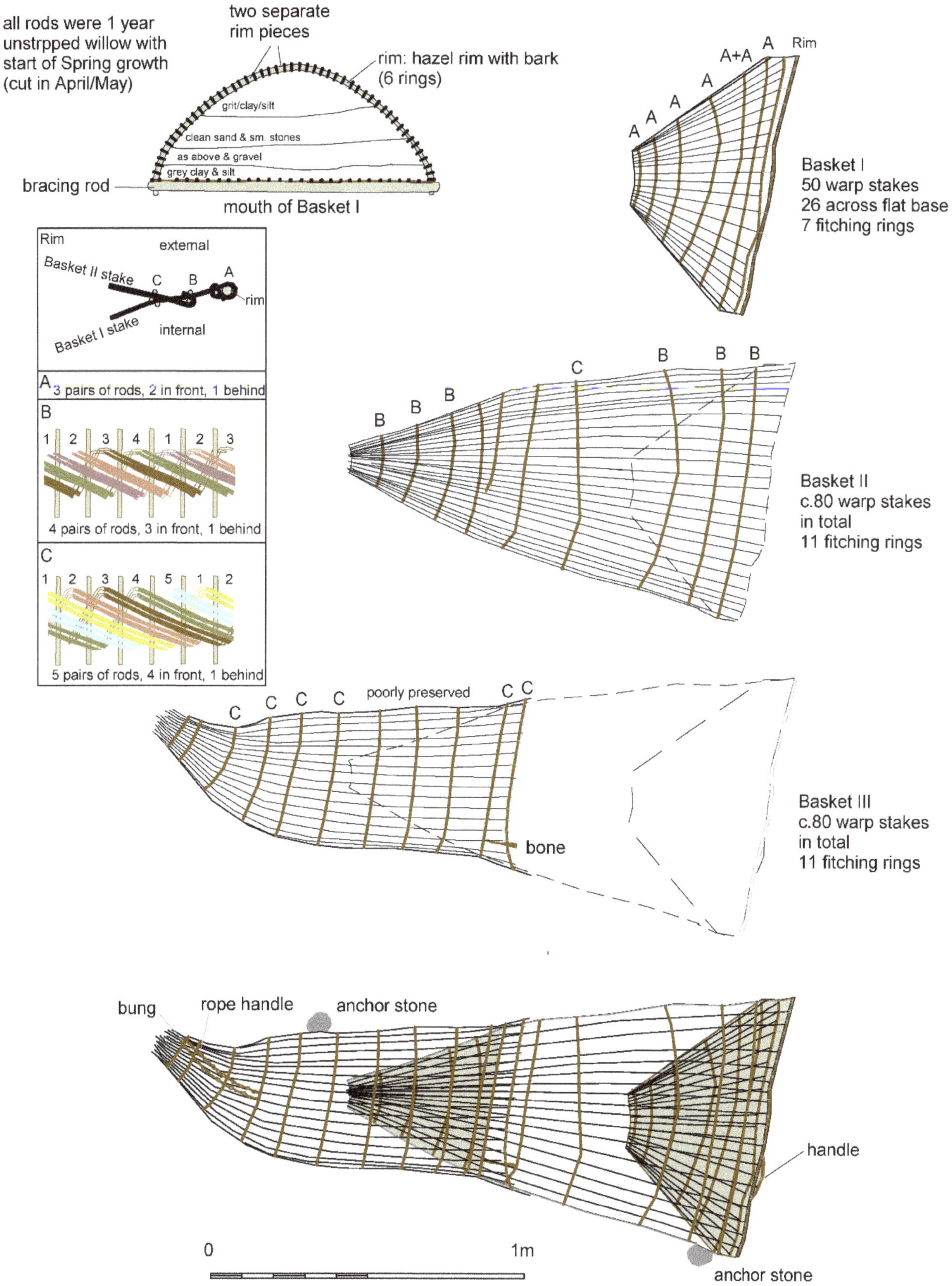

all rods were 1 year
unstrpped willow with
start of Spring growth
(cut in April/May)

two separate
rim pieces

rim: hazel rim with bark
(6 rings)

grit/clay/silt

clean sand & sm. stones

as above & gravel

grey clay & silt

bracing rod

mouth of Basket I

A+A A Rim

A
A
A
A
A A

Basket I
50 warp stakes
26 across flat base
7 fitching rings

Rim

Basket II stake

external

C B A

rim

Basket I stake

internal

A 3 pairs of rods, 2 in front, 1 behind

B

1 2 3 4 1 2 3

4 pairs of rods, 3 in front, 1 behind

C

1 2 3 4 5 1 2

5 pairs of rods, 4 in front, 1 behind

B B B
C
B B
B
B

Basket II
c.80 warp stakes
in total
11 fitching rings

C C C C   poorly preserved   C C

bone

Basket III
c.80 warp stakes
in total
11 fitching rings

bung   rope handle   anchor stone

handle

0   1m

anchor stone

Figure 62: The construction of the Eel Basket SF50.

Figure 63: Wicker Eel Basket SF50.

Figure 65: Following the removal of the outer 'shell' it was possible to see the 'non-return valve' baskets within.

Figure 64: Side view of SF50. Note the anchor stone woven into the lower (right hand) end of the basket.

Figure 66: Side view of the 'non-return valve' baskets within SF50.

Figure 67: Basket I: note Basket II inserted into Basket I just below the third (from left) fitching ring and twisted back to attach to the second ring.

Figure 68: The woven handle at the end of the basket. The handle was removed to open the basket to release the catch.

of waling and then into Basket I between hoops 2 and 3 (the first being the rigid rim). The stakes were then folded back over hoop 2 (Figure 62, inset 'Rim'). Basket II was 500mm in diameter at the mouth and the stakes were again drawn together with a total of 11 waling rings, to form a terminus that was 90mm wide. Both 4 and 5 rod waling was used to form the rings (Figure 62) although some rings were too desiccated to record.

Half way down Basket II a 110mm long bone was identified. The bone was a complete and well-preserved dog ulna, which produced an estimated shoulder height of 0.45m, using Harcourt's (1974) calculation. When fleshed,

the ulna is paired with the radius and the absence of this bone may suggest that the bone was washed in, rather than deliberately deposited as bait.

The yellow eel is a carnivorous fish and smaller bottle eel traps would be baited. However, the silver eel stops eating and such bait would be superfluous (though traps were sometimes baited, possibly reflecting the lack of physiological knowledge by the medieval fishing folk; Cooper 2003). A dog foreleg would be an unusual form of bait: the dog is not usually a food animal and it may make more sense to bait the trap with more readily available butchered stock animals or, more likely, fish.

Figure 69: Integral handle at the rim of Basket SF50.

Figure 71: Detail showing how anchor stone Sample 111 was woven on to the main basket.

Figure 70: right, Lower half of Basket II drawn to a virtual point. The small anchor stone (Sample 110) weighing down the basket is bottom left.

On completion of Basket II, Basket III was added (Figure 62). Basket III was remarkably similar to Basket II being 1.4m long by 500mm wide at the mouth. It was also constructed of *c.* 80 warp stakes and 11 fitching rings. The terminus, however, had been drawn tightly shut with a twisted rope and bung/peg that was removable (to release the catch).

Finally, two anchor stones (small stones that were waisted in the middle) were attached to the basket by

twisted withy ties (Figures 71–72) to weigh the basket down. The anchor stone towards the mouth of the basket (Sample 111) was identified (Dr. R. Clements, Geology Department, University of Leicester, pers. com.) as a "worn, well-cemented sandstone (quartz grains cemented by quartz) probably collected from the gravel tills and selected for its natural waisting and appropriate size". The anchor stone towards the terminus was identified as "fine to medium grained sandstone. Carbonaceous patches and likely to be from the Coal Measures. Worked to waisted shape". The anchor stones were small in relation to the size of the basket (Figure 63) and it seems probable that the basket must also have been secured in the water by additional means.

Eel Basket SF41: the remains of a second large 'openwork' eel basket were located on top of the weir (between Posts 325, 368 and 369). It was severely machine damaged but survived as the base of a basket, with fragments of two inner baskets (the 'non-return valves') just visible (Figure 73). It measured 1.5m long by 0.55m wide at the mouth. Although the rim was missing it was likely to have been near-complete as, assuming it was of a similar construction to Basket SF50, there were indications of all three baskets surviving and again, two anchor stones were identified.

Figure 72: Four anchor stones from the eel baskets. Left two from Basket SF50 (upper is Sample 110, lower is 111), right two from Basket SF41 (upper is Sample 112, lower is Sample 113).

Figure 73: The less well-preserved Basket SF41, located on top of the weir. The mouth of the basket is to the left of the picture, facing north.

The stakes of Basket SF41 were made from one year old willow withies, all less than 15mm apart. The stakes were supported by at least 23 'hoops' of woven withies, although it was not clear which hoops belonged to which basket within the construction. The pattern of the hoops was difficult to determine but of the hoops that survived well it could be seen that some, at least, were constructed as two pairs of withies plainly woven (in/out/in/out) but each pair woven alternately. Towards the terminus the same pattern was used but with single withy rods.

The two anchor stones associated with Basket SF41 were both found beneath the basket: Stone Sample 112 near the mouth, 113 near the terminus (Figure 72). Dr R. Clements identified Sample 112 as being "Fine to medium grained sandstone. Some micaceous fragments, 'Pitting' may be fossil roots. Almost definitely Coal Measure Sandstone". Sample 113 was "Medium grained quartzite sandstone. Likely to be from a different source to the other anchor stone samples".

Brushwood Bundles

To the south of the platform hurdle panel (364), but lying over the stones and even up on the weir itself were a number of groups of brushwood twigs. Most were quite fragmentary and difficult to record. None was obviously tied but the great number of aligned sticks suggests they were deliberately placed bundles of brushwood. The bundles may have formed part of the platform structure, possibly used as levelling material or perhaps, more likely, served as eel tufts similar to those recorded at HL5.

One metre south of the platform, up against the weir (near Post 300) the better surviving bundles were given the context numbers 337, 338 and 339 (Figure 38):

Bundle 337 (also SF42) lay up on the weir, to the south of Post 369 and at the terminus end of Basket SF41. It was aligned north-west to south-east, 0.35m x 0.2m, and consisted of some very fine twigs. There was no obvious tie around the bundle but the brushwood withies were all aligned and tightly packed suggesting they once were.

Bundle 338 lay on the stone platform, was aligned north-east to south-west, 1m x 0.35m and was again made up of thin wispy roundwood twigs.

Bundle 339 also lay on the weir platform, was aligned north-west to south-east, 1m x 0.6m and lay slightly below bundle 338

Anchor Stones

Three large 'anchor stones' were found in the vicinity of HL12. Anchor stones are large waisted stones, unique to Hemington Quarry (Salisbury 1991a; Salisbury and Brown 2009) thought to be weights for either fish traps, nets or possibly boats. Their large size suggests they could not easily have been lifted in and out of the water suggesting they perhaps provided permanent 'stations' to attach traps to.

Anchor Stone SF37 was found towards the northern end of the weir just behind the upright Panel 376 (Figure 41), near the top of the weir (29.00m AOD). It was Bromsgrove Sandstone, 0.51m long by 0.35m x 0.20m wide and weighed 51kg. It was very water worn with degraded pick marks in the grooves.

Anchor Stone SF38 was only located as 'from HL12' but was recorded as Bromsgrove Sandstone, 43.1kg, 0.52m long by 0.31 x 0.22m wide. It was also water worn but with sharper pick marks in the grooves.

Anchor Stone SF39 was located downstream of the south end of the weir, near the area of higher Holme Pierrepont sands (5m SE of T341). SF39 was Bromsgrove Sandstone, 47.2kg, 0.49m long by 0.30m x 0.22m. It was water worn but still retained pick marks in the grooves.

Mill Stones/Millstone Roughouts

Seven fragments of millstone roughouts were recovered from the HL12 weir, re-used as infill to the weir (Figure 74 & Table 4). All were of Derbyshire Millstone Grit

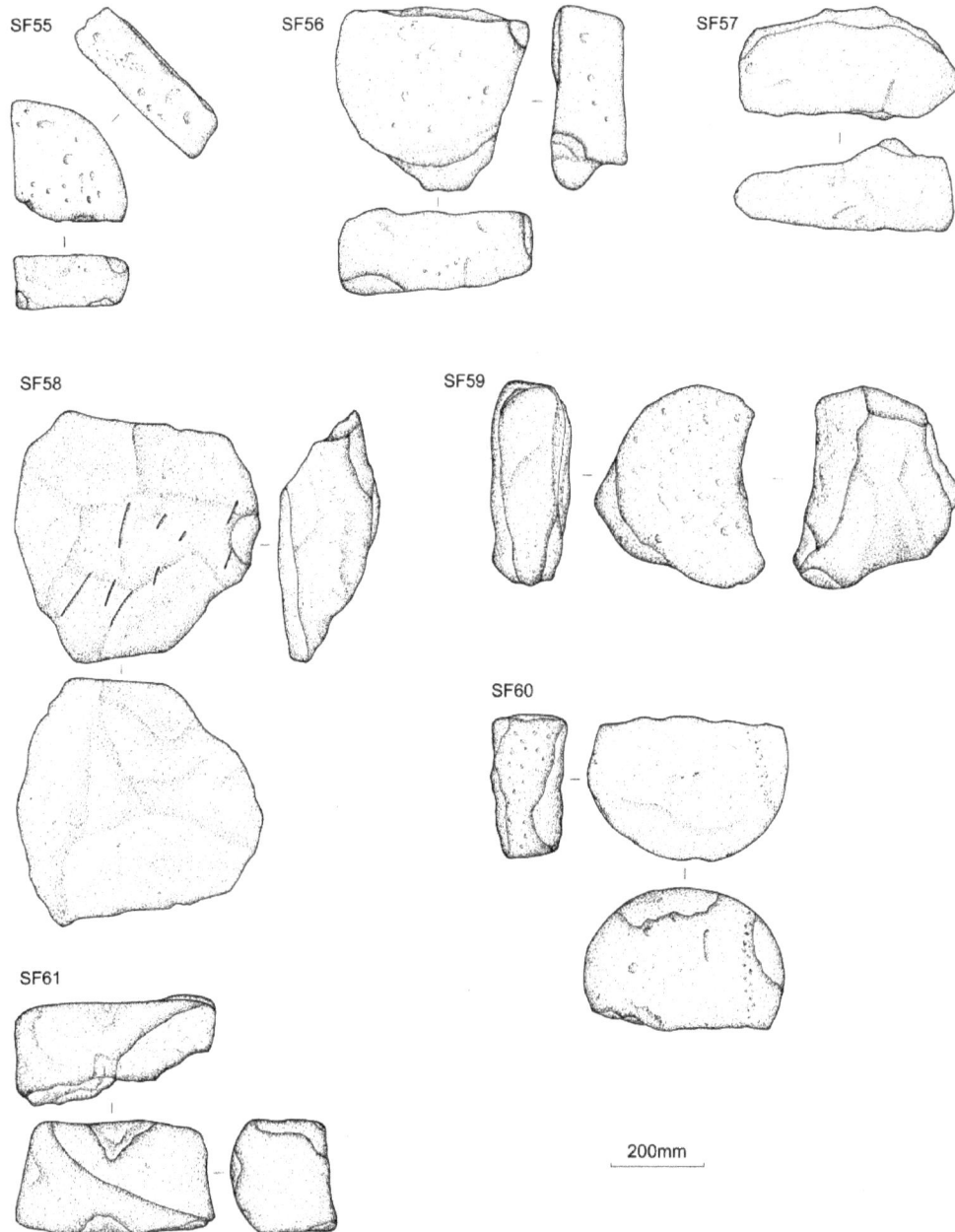

Figure 74: The millstone roughout fragments from HL12.

Table 4: Mill stone attributes

Small find number	Approximate radius (mm)	Approximate thickness near centre (mm)	Comment
SF55	220	110	A quarter millstone with part cut central spindle hole. Pebble imprints on the surface.
SF56	450	160	A very rough quarter millstone. One good curving edge and the beginnings of a central hole. Pebble imprints.
SF57	-	200	Very broken roughout consisting only of one slightly curving edge.
SF58	520	220	Again, just the beginnings of a roughout. One slightly curving edge and the start of a central spindle hole.
SF59	250	160	Over half with a curved edge and the very beginnings of a central spindle hole.
SF60	210	160	The most complete circle but with no central hole.
SF61	-	170	Very rough with only one slightly curving edge.

(C. Salisbury pers. comm.). None was even approaching completeness but the range in diameter of approximately 0.42m – 1.4m suggests they were large and intended for a powered mill. Many of the roughouts had pitted surfaces made by pebble imprints, suggesting the stone may not have been of a suitable quality for use as a grinding stone.

Mill Paddles

In the 2km stretch of the River Trent downstream from HL12 seven mill paddles have been found. Although none was directly associated with HL12, as wooden objects that float they are likely to have originated from either the 1985 mill dam site or from the HL12 weir/former mill site. A full description of the mill paddles has therefore been included in this report as Appendix I.

Leather Artefacts (Nicholas J. Cooper)

A total of eight fragments of leather (grouped under five small finds numbers) was recovered. The group includes a complete shoe sole (Small Find no. 43), two fragments of shoe sole (SFs 44 and 46), and a tasselled fragment (SF49). All were recovered from stone weir site HL12, the construction of which is dated to *c.* 1125AD.

SF43 was a complete shoe sole from right foot with narrow rounded toe (Figure 75). Although none of the uppers remain, the shoe was of turnshoe construction of York Type 2 with an edge/flesh stitch around the sole (Mould *et al.* 2003, 3269, fig.1592). The shape of the sole, which has a distinct waist and an oval rather than pointed toe, corresponds to York Type D2 of 12th–13th century date (Mould *et al.* 2003, 3269, fig.1594). Length 278mm, width at seat 68mm, width of waist 40mm width of tread 85mm. Length is equivalent to adult size 7 or 8 (Allin 1981, 23).

The shoe, or ankle boot, to which this sole belonged, clearly had a long and hard life, as is normal at this

period. The sole has two large wear holes, one towards the outside of the heel seat and one on the tread, towards the outside of the foot at the base of the short toes, rather than on the ball of the foot at the base of the big toe; suggesting the individual walked with an out-turned foot. A circle of tunnel stitching holes on the bottom (grain side) of the sole indicates that the hole was patched to form a 'clump' repair, and the patch has since detached, and similarly, a line of tunnel stitch holes across the waist of the sole and around the inside edge of the seat indicates that a heel clump repair was also undertaken. Two oblique knife cuts also emanate from the area of the worn area on the tread and extend beyond the area covered by the clump, suggesting they may have occurred subsequently.

The turnshoe construction is the most common technique of shoe making throughout the medieval period. Essentially the shoe is made inside-out by sewing the edge (lasting margin) of upper to the edge of the sole and then turning it the right way round so that (as in this case) the seam is on the inside and the smooth grain surface of the leather is on the outside with the flesh side forming the insole (Allin 1981, 22). At York, the Type 2 edge/flesh seam (as here) emerged as the standard construction technique from the end of the 12th century until the later 15th century, the sole shape indicating that this example probably dates to the 12th or 13th century and was deposited not long after the construction of the stone weir into which it became ensnared (Figure 38).

SF44 was a very worn fragment of a sole from a shoe of turnshoe construction for which the exact nature of the stitch cannot be ascertained due to wear of the edge. One original rounded edge either from a large heel seat or a rounded tread. Other two edges straight but worn flat. Tunnel stitching apparent on grain side along these two edges and on the flesh side on the curved edge, indicates that the fragment had been reused as a clump repair piece. Preserved length 67mm, preserved width 64mm.

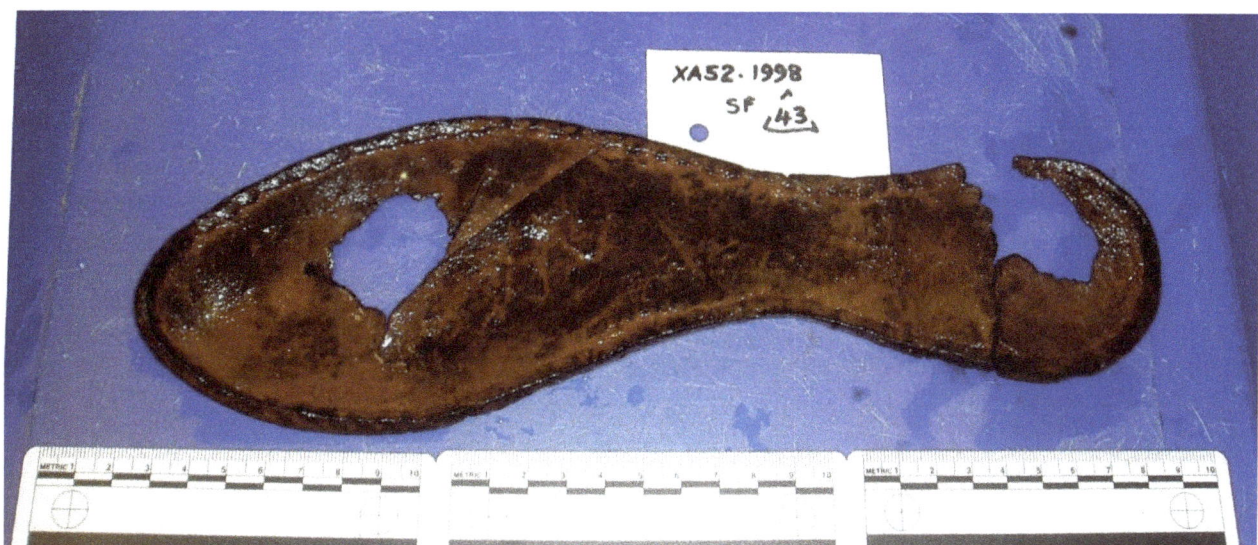

Figure 75: Complete shoe sole SF43, found downstream from Plank 365 on the HL12 weir.

SF45 consisted of four, small irregular fragments of shoe sole, indicated by worn surfaces at edge of grain. Length of largest fragment 46mm.

SF46 was a very worn fragment of heel seat from a turnshoe. Stitching is apparent on flesh side but too worn to ascertain exact form. Width of heal seat estimated at 68mm (60mm preserved).

SF49 was a polygonal fragment with tasselled edge, created by parallel knife cuts across the majority of the surface, leaving a 10mm wide margin along the top three edges (Figure 76). The end of the tassels are obliquely squared off, but longer and tapered at one side. Length 70mm, width 72mm, thickness 4mm.

Tasselled pieces are known from straps possibly used to suspend scabbards dating to the 14th century (Mould *et al.* 2003, 3367, fig.1691.15612) and on decorated belts such as those also from York (Mould *et al.* 2003, 3394, fig.1714.15888). The thickness of the piece certainly suggests it could support weight and is similar to the York examples. There is however, no means of attachment apparent for this fragment so it may just represent an offcut.

Tree-Ring Dating of HL12 (Robert Howard)

One hundred and thirty-eight timber numbers were issued during the excavation of HL12, including hurdle panels and sundry stray timbers. Ninety-nine timbers were either posts or jointed timbers (such as planks or baseplates) and of these, 24 were identified as being not oak. Of the 75 remaining oak timbers 65 were sampled for dendrochronological analysis. Thirty-four of the larger timbers were cut with a chainsaw (by the Nottingham Tree Ring Dating Laboratory) and the remainder sampled with a hand saw by ULAS site staff. The analysis programme was delayed for almost a decade and during this time the larger chain sawed samples have unfortunately been mislaid. The results below are therefore restricted to the smaller timbers, cut by hand saw.

Thirty-one samples from HL12 were analysed. Nine were not suitable and were not measured; 22 measured. Of the 22 measured samples 15 were grouped and dated, five measured, grouped but undated (300, 306, 311, 316 and 317) and two ungrouped and undated (313 and 318).

The locations of the analysed samples are illustrated in Figure 77.

Of the timbers that could be dated samples were available from both upstream and downstream rows of posts, and both large and small posts were represented (detailed above in Figure 77). Five timbers had absolute felling dates ranging from 1116 – 1120, and all the dated timbers from HL12 could have been felled within those years, assuming 15–50 sapwood rings. There were insufficient samples to suggest phased construction of the weir, and it is conceivable that either there was a four year collection period or that it took

Figure 76: Tasselled-edged leather fragment, SF49.

at least four years to construct. In the absence of the large mill timber samples it is currently only possible to say that the weir was probably constructed around 1120, with a likelihood that it was constructed in one phase.

Dendrochronological dating of the rows of posts associated with the mill dam excavated in 1985 (Figure 1; Clay and Salisbury 1990) suggest felling in the first half of the 12th century; the best dates were PL1-58 (a horizontal timber on the upstream face of the dam), possible complete sap, felled soon after 1063 and PL4-201 (*ex situ* post) felled sometime between 1102 and 1137. The remainder did not include heart/sap boundaries.

Function of HL12

The structure bears close resemblance to the mill dam recorded in 1985 in having a submerged dam or weir with a possible sluice structure to raise and control a head of water (Clay and Salisbury 1990, Figure 61). There are also similarities in the timber jointing of the 12th century tidal watermill at Greenwich in London (Davis 2009, Figure 61) where a grid of baseplates appeared to support a plank floor. Mill sites were often host to fishing activities, particularly eels, finely illustrated in the 14th century Luttrell Psalter (British Library, Figure 78) which depicts eel baskets set in the race stream of a water mill. Much of the evidence for milling, the monumental timber baseplates suggesting large-scale water management, the scattered mill paddles downstream (see Appendix I) and the millstone roughouts re-used in the weir infill, suggest that a mill once occupied the site, but had been destroyed and re-worked into the weir. Definite evidence for fishing, the weir, the funnelling of the flow, the brushwood bundles and the large eel baskets, suggest the structure might be interpreted as one of the more substantial 'fixed engine' fishery sites, mentioned in medieval documents (Losco-Bradley and Salisbury 1979). It seems likely that this is synonymous with the Anglo-Saxon *cytwera* or basket weirs, but it is has proved impossible to find archaeological parallels.

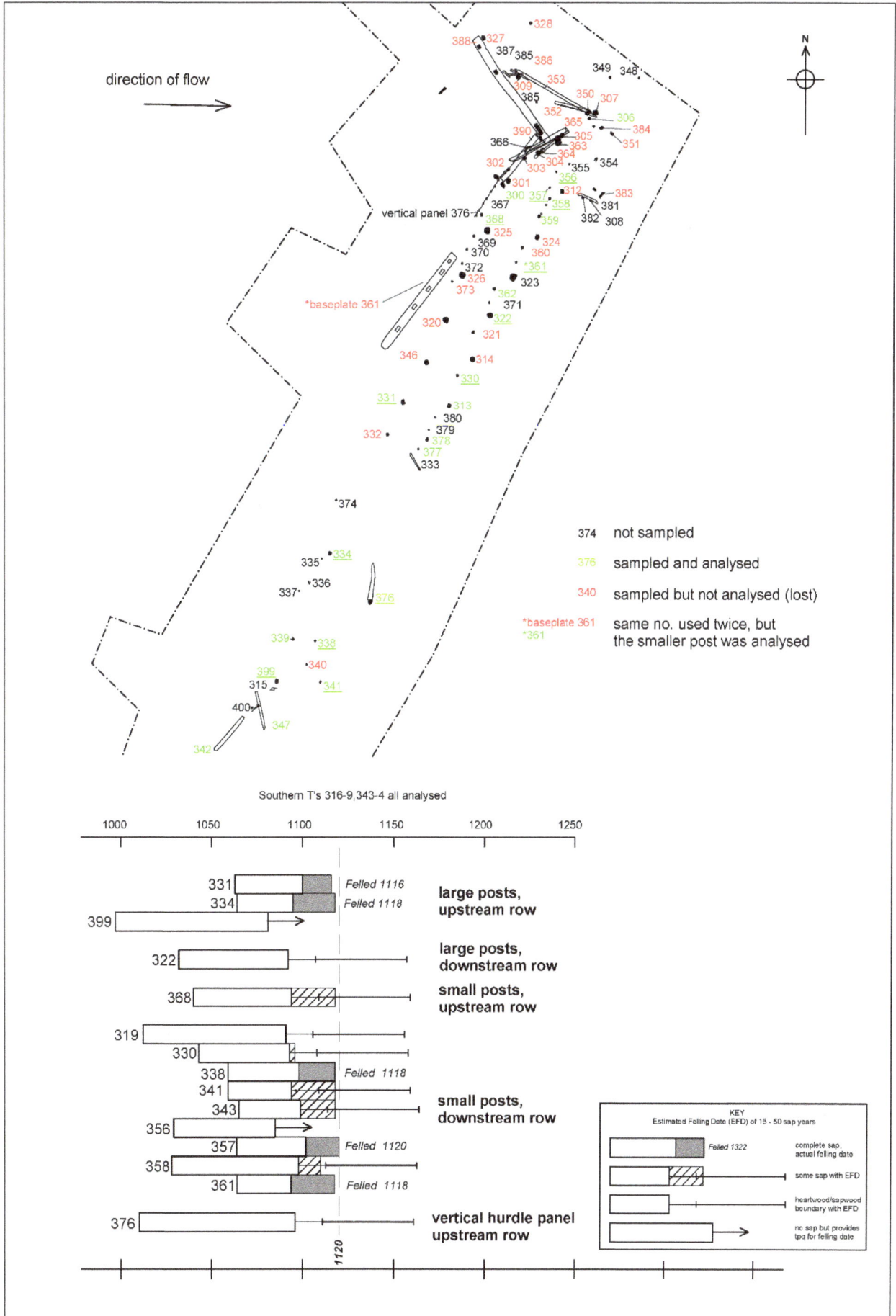

Figure 77: Plan showing timbers sampled for dendrochronological analysis (including the locations of the lost samples). Dated timber sample numbers are underlined.

Figure 78: Illustration of a watermill from the Luttrell Psalter (The British Library). Note the long wicker eel baskets in the head race waters.

5

Jetty Structures (HL6, 8, 9, 10, 11 & 13)

Six examples of jetty structures were recorded from the right bank of the medieval channel immediately downstream of the HL12 weir. All of the structures were within the medieval parish of Castle Donington. Following Salisbury (1985) these have been previously reported as 'shoot' structures (Cooper and Ripper 2000; 2001; Cooper 2003). Salisbury (1985) described surviving 18th century 'shoots' along the Trent, these being bank-side works of stone and timber designed to protect the banks from erosion (their name derived from the local waterman vernacular). It is suggested that the jetty structures served as cribs (*sensu* Seebohm 1905, 153) structures placed into the channel to facilitate a scour pool and produce eddies thereby attracting salmonids. Of course they could also have served as landing stages and as fishing platforms.

Site HL6

HL6 was formed by two lines of oak piles projecting from the river bank effectively forming a jetty of triangular plan, enclosing 8.8m², which was infilled with large sandstone blocks and brushwood (Figures 79–80). The stone blocks had been laid in crude courses inside the triangular crib, sloping up the bank of the river to a height of *c.* 2m (*c.* 29m AOD)

The stones at the base of the structure against the upstream face were retained by an oak plank (at 27.7m AOD). The partial remains of another plank were discovered just outside of the downstream face and probably represent the remains of a similar revetment plank.

Seven *in situ* pile posts were associated with HL6. The four posts making the western revetment of the crib were roughly 1.40m apart, while the eastern revetment posts were slightly closer together at *c.* 1.10m. All the posts were oak, had eroded tops and, excepting T36, were quarter conversions. Tree ring samples were cut from the posts *in situ* but Post 36 was lifted whole. Post 36 appeared to have been squared (possibly to remove planks from two sides of the trunk) with two different sizes of saw-marks recorded; a larger set of marks that were 10–14mm apart and a smaller set 3–5mm apart. The smaller set is likely to have been produced by the same saw used at a much slower speed, perhaps cutting through a denser area of wood. The larger saw-marks appeared to indicate a saw with 2 1/2 teeth per inch, a large rip saw with a narrow 'set' to the teeth, used to coarsely rip through large areas of timber. The post was then dressed with evidence of axe blades (40mm+ wide) down two chamfered corners of the post.

Figure 79: HL6 looking south. Vertical scales: 1m, horizontal scales: 2m.

49

Plan of HL6

Trent palaeochannel

N

T39

T38

T40

T37

T36

T41

riverbank

large blocks of
Bromsgrove sandstone,
no tooling marks observed

brushwood

T42

0
5m

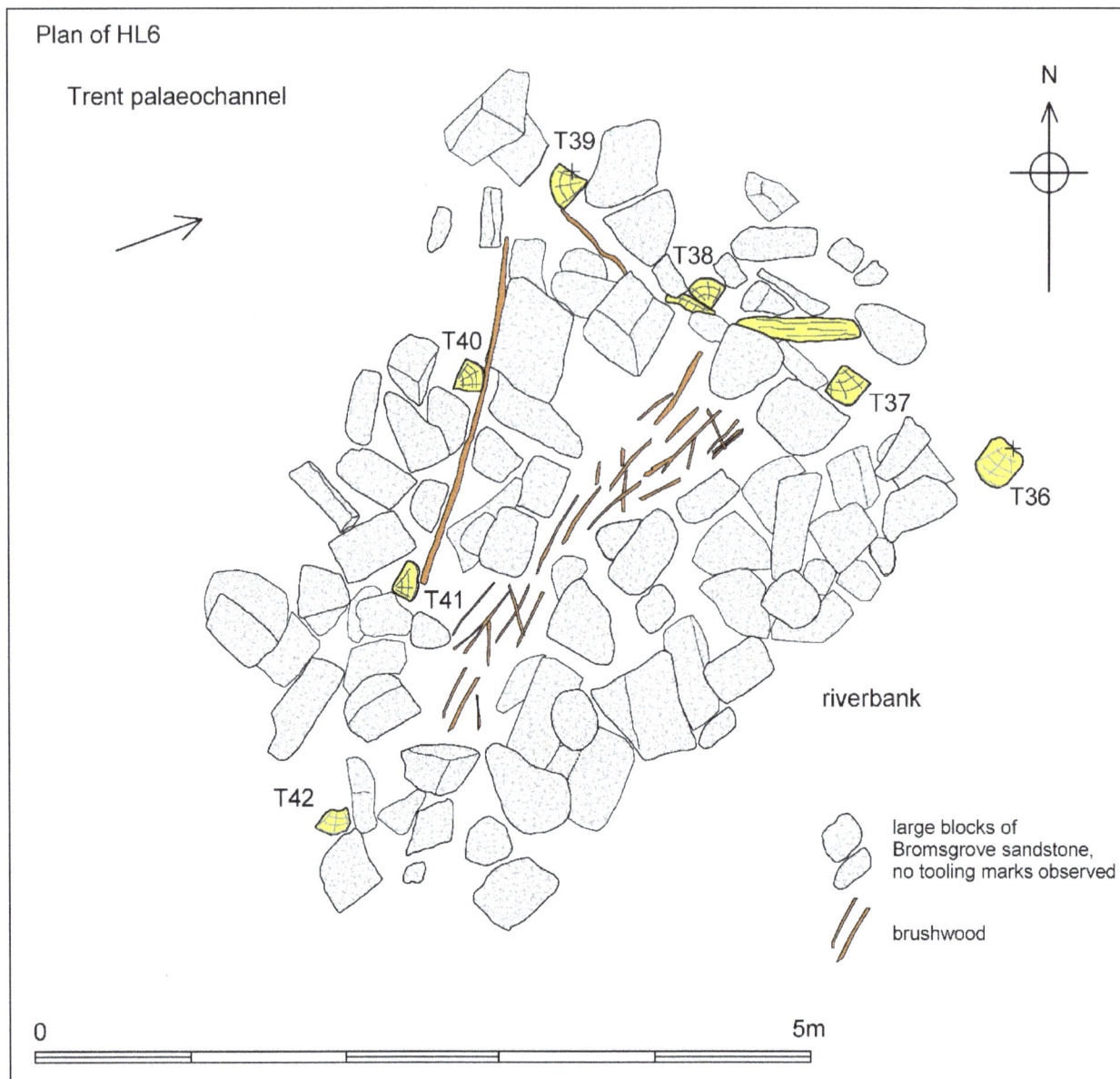

Northeast facing section through HL6

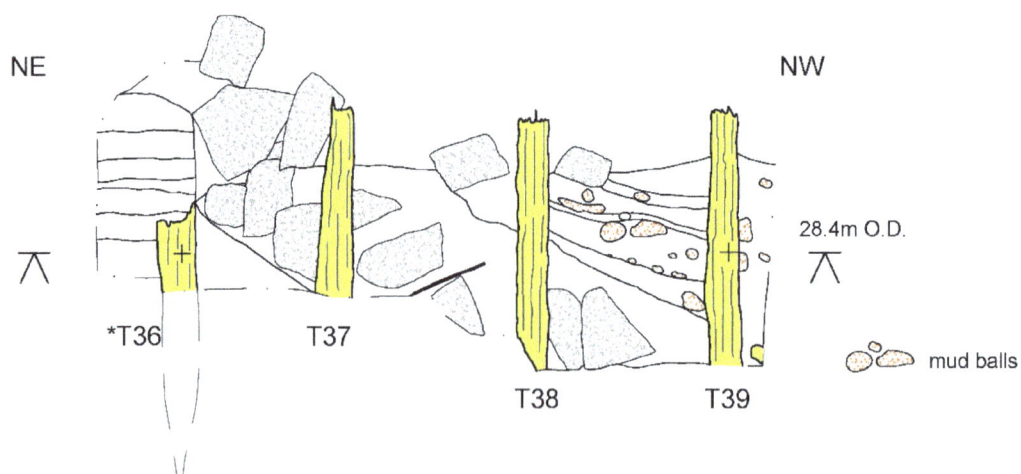

NE

NW

28.4m O.D.

*T36
T37

T38
T39

mud balls

Figure 80: Plan and section through HL6.

Two timber planks were also located within HL6. T44 formed the lower course of the horizontal revetment of the western edge of the structure and appeared to have been sprung from behind Post 41 and kinked to lie behind Post 40 (Figure 80). It was tangentially split, 2.4m long by 0.34 x 0.05m wide but eroded and split along its length. Plank 43 was a loose, fragmentary piece, 0.7m long by 0.21 x 0.02m.

Limited excavation of the stone core revealed a mass of brushwood, some with evident chop marks. The brushwood was found within a matrix of silty clay which was probably deposited by water flowing through the structure. This is reminiscent of some of William Jessop's 18th century 'waterworks', the use of brushwood kidweirs that encouraged silt or 'warp' to deposit around the structure and thereby stabilise it (Salisbury 1985 and pers. comm.).

All seven of the posts were sampled for tree ring analysis but only two produced a date. T42 had 10 sap rings and a final ring date of 1290, T38 had a heartwood/sapwood boundary of 1272 (estimated felling date of 1287–1322). Both have First Measured Ring Dates that fall within the range observed in structures HL8 and 10. HL8 has a suggested construction date of after 1325 and HL10 of after 1315. It is perhaps likely that HL6 was constructed concurrently with HL10.

Site HL8

Another jetty, HL8, was also constructed of a timber frame with stone infill (Table 5 & Figure 81). Deep scouring around the foundations had caused the partial collapse of the structure in to a scour pool, leading to the rare survival of timbers with their joints.

Table 5: Table of HL8 timbers

Timber no.	Location	Joints/tool marks	Dimensions	Date
		Posts, *in situ*		
246	eastern edge of shoot, on the bankside	top eroded in antiquity	250 x 14mm by 1.06m length quarter conversion	not sampled
247	western edge of shoot, on the bankside	top eroded in antiquity	230 x 210mm, length unknown quarter conversion	70 rings, did not date
248	1.5m SW of T246	top eroded in antiquity	200 x 100mm, length unknown quarter conversion	felling date 1325
252	2m north of T246	top eroded in antiquity	220 x 110mm, Length unknown half conversion	did not date
		Posts, *ex situ*		
244	machine excavated, near HL8	pile post (tapered at one end). Pit saw marks	220 x 120mm, 3.08m length half timber, rectangular	18 sap rings, LMR 1319
245	machine excavated, near HL8	pile post (tapered at one end). saw marks on chamfered corners	240 x 110mm, 2.87m length half timber, D-shaped section	h/s boundary, LMR 1300
		Posts with tenon at one end		
249	machine excavated, near HL8	central tenon (220 x 70mm) with asymmetric shoulders and off-centre dowel hole.	330mm diameter 3.57 m length whole timber, chamfered square	14 sap rings, LMR 1286
251	horizontal, *c.* 1m north of shoot structure	asymmetric tenon (215 x 70mm), sloping dowel hole	210 x 180mm 3.40m length quarter conversion	felling date 1322
254	horizontal, NE base of shoot structure	tenon (180 x 40mm) with asymmetric shoulders	180 x 160mm 3.50m length almost whole, one square edge	did not date
255	horizontal, immediately south of post 246 & the post stain (poss. derived from stain) on riverbank side.	asymmetric tenon (190 x 60mm), rounded & tapered tip but no dowel.	180 x 70 mm 3.00m length Quarter conversion	felling date 1322
258	machine excavated, near HL8	tenon (200 x 60mm) with one very narrow shoulder (20mm) the other 100mm wide. No dowel	170 x 210mm 3.07m length quarter conversion	no h/s LMR 1285

Table 5 *continued*

Timber no.	Location	Joints/tool marks	Dimensions	Date
		Beams/whole trunks		
250	near top of stones on eastern edge of main platform	?felling wedge at one end. Large side-branches removed.	500mm diameter 2.50m length whole trunk	felling date 1324
253	at base of stones (below water table) along western edge of platform	?branch, chopped to cone shape at one end, other end has notch joint cut out of a wedge.	440 x 320mm 3m length Whole	not sampled
		Timbers with mortices		
241	machine excavated, near HL8	split & broken but rectangular 'plank' with steps cut into edge face. Poss. broken mortices	300 x 170mm 1.53m length over-quarter conversion	h/s boundary LMR1302
242	machine excavated, near HL8	worn, battered rect. Timber with at least 3 mortices mort 1 = 220 x 80mm+ mort 2 = 300 x 110mm+ mort 3 = 240 x 100mm+ 1.2m apart at furthest	290 x 160mm 2.82m length over-quarter conversion	No h/s boundary LMR 1239
243	machine excavated, near HL8	D-shaped cross section. mort 1 = 320 x 110mm mort 2 = 290 x 110mm 1.50m apart	360 x 160mm 3.20m length Half conversion	98 rings did not date
256	at base of stones (below water table) along western edge of platform	mort 1 = 240 x 100mm mort 2 = 220 x 100mm 1.58m apart	320 x 170mm 5.2m length quarter conversion	h/s boundary LMR 1267
257	below T256	mort 1 = ? x 110mm mort 2 = 360 x 110mm 2.68m apart	240 x 160mm 3.80m length quarter conversion	No h/s boundary LMR 1259

Eighteen timbers were associated with HL8 (Figure 82). Four posts were observed *in situ* (Timbers 246, 248, 252 and 247) with a fifth located by a post stain. A further seven posts were located in the immediate vicinity of HL8 (Timbers 244, 245, 249, 251, 254, 255 and 258) and are likely to have been derived from it. Five of these posts had roughly cut tenons at one end and were tapered, to be driven, at the other end. Most of the tenons were not central to the cross-section of the timber (Figure 83, top left), and often the shoulders were not cut to the same height on either side. Two of the tenons had dowel peg holes through the broad face, but again the holes were not central to the tenon. All tenons were roughly shaped with an axe: smooth finishes do not appear to have been thought necessary (Figure 83, top right).

Five timbers had at least two through mortice holes (241, 242, 243, 256 and 257). The distances between the mortice holes varied, but of the three better preserved beams two (Timbers 243 and 256) had mortices that were *c.* 1.5m apart and the third (Timber 257) was 2.68m apart. These distances can also be found between the *in situ* post (for example Posts 246 and 248 are 1.5m apart, 248 and 252 are 2.5m apart). The three beams were notably not straight timbers: all were bent and had numerous side branches removed. The mortice holes were all rectangular, consistently around 110mm wide and between 220–360mm long. All could have housed the tenons, albeit a loose fit. Some of the mortices (both from T256 and one from T257)

also had peg holes through the side of the joint, presumably to secure the tenon.

A further two unconverted trunks were also recorded on HL8. Trunk 250 appeared to have been placed behind *in situ* Posts 248 and 252, thereby forming the horizontal element of the eastern revetment of the crib. It lay directly on the natural gravel bank of the river with its lower end at *c.* 28m AOD and upper end at *c.* 29m AOD. The trunk had a felling wedge at one end, with a large side-branch having been removed immediately above the cut. It may have been grown in an open aspect, such as a hedgerow or parkland, and appears to have been selected for its bulk: the knots and large side-branches may have precluded conversion into a timber. Gravel and large stones had tumbled over T250, perhaps indicating that an upper revetment timber had been lost during the collapse of the structure.

Trunk 253 mirrored T250 and formed the western revetment of the crib. It was not obviously associated with any *in situ* upright posts although it lay slightly deeper than the lower end of T250, suggesting scouring had been deeper along the western side. Timbers 256 (with mortices) and 254 (tenoned) were also found in a similar location suggesting the calamitous collapse of a jointed structure. Timber 253 was cross-cut with an axe at one end. The other end had a felling wedge, which had then had a notch cut out of it (see sketch on Figure 81). The notch appears to have been

T254

T256

Trent palaeochannel

N

felling
wedge

notch cut
into wedge

T257

PP North

T249

T251

T252

T253

PP West

T247

PP East

T246

post
stain

T250

T248

T255

gravel terrace
(riverbank)

PP South

0

5m

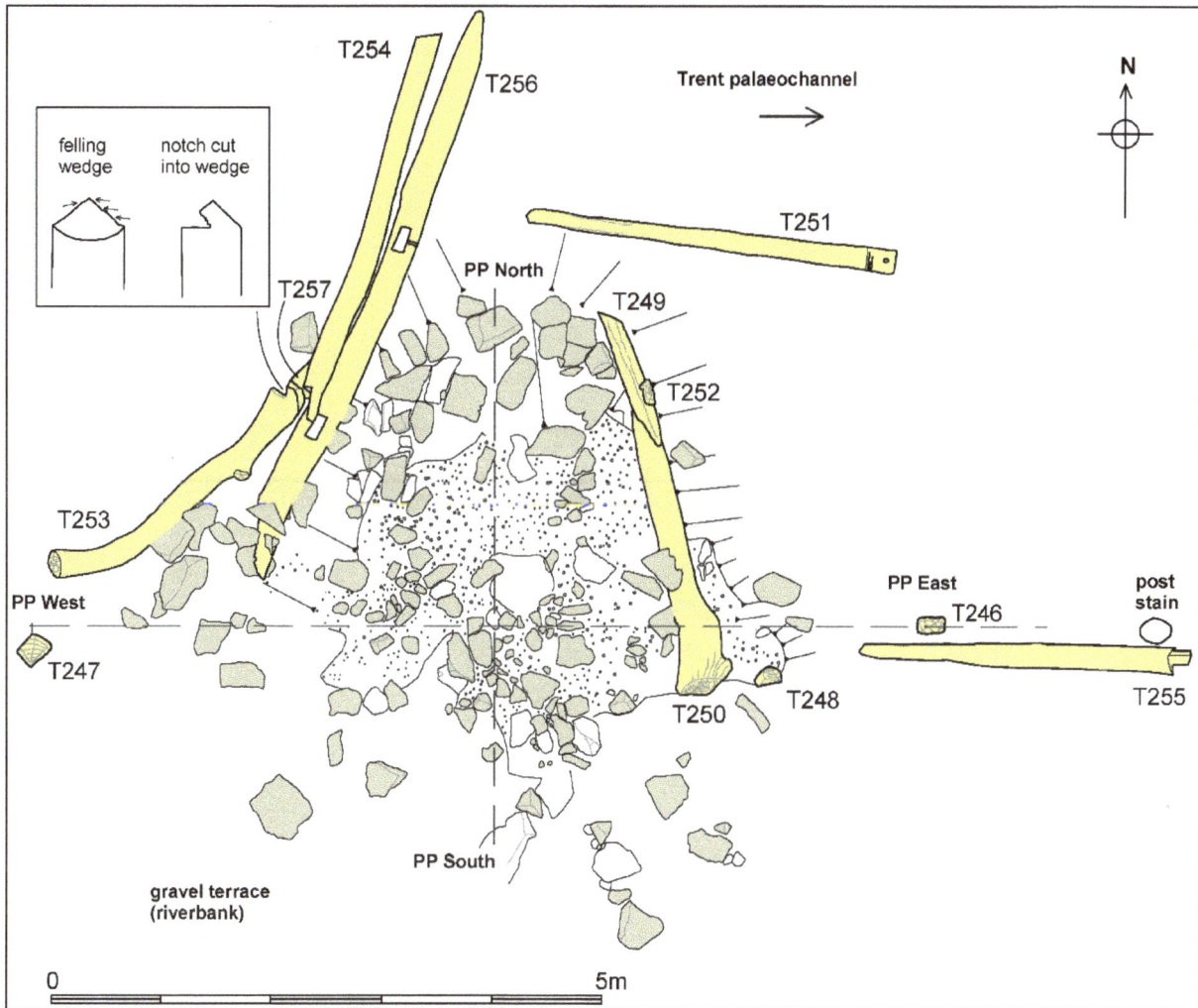

North/South section through HL8

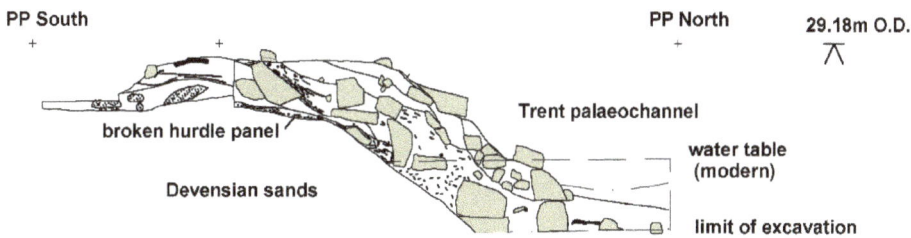

PP South

PP North

29.18m O.D.

Trent palaeochannel

broken hurdle panel

water table
(modern)

Devensian sands

limit of excavation

East/West section through HL8

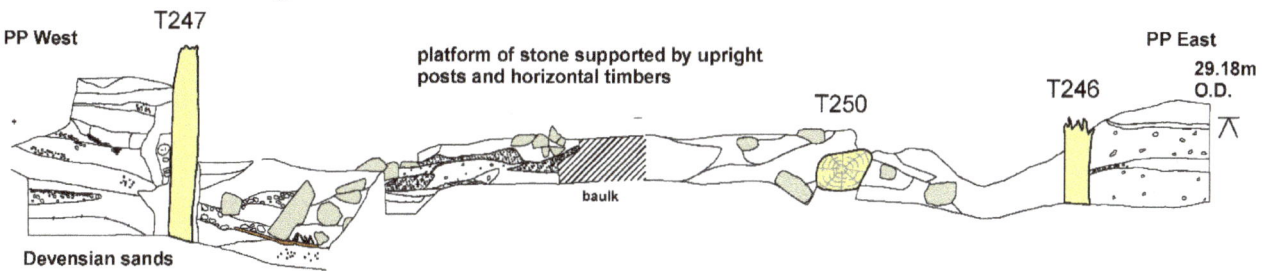

T247

PP West

platform of stone supported by upright
posts and horizontal timbers

PP East

29.18m
O.D.

T250

T246

baulk

Devensian sands

Figure 81: Plan of riverbank Jetty Structure HL8 with N-S and E-W cross-sections below.

HL8 upright posts

Timber 244   Timber 245   Timber 249

3m

18 sapwood
rings
LMR 1319

h/s boundary
LMR 1300

14 sawood rings
LMR 1286

pit saw
marks

0

Timber 251   Timber 254   Timber 255   Timber 258

3m

complete sapwood
(22 rings)
Felling date 1322

not
measured

complete sapwood
(22 rings)
Felling date 1322

no h/s
LMR 1285

0

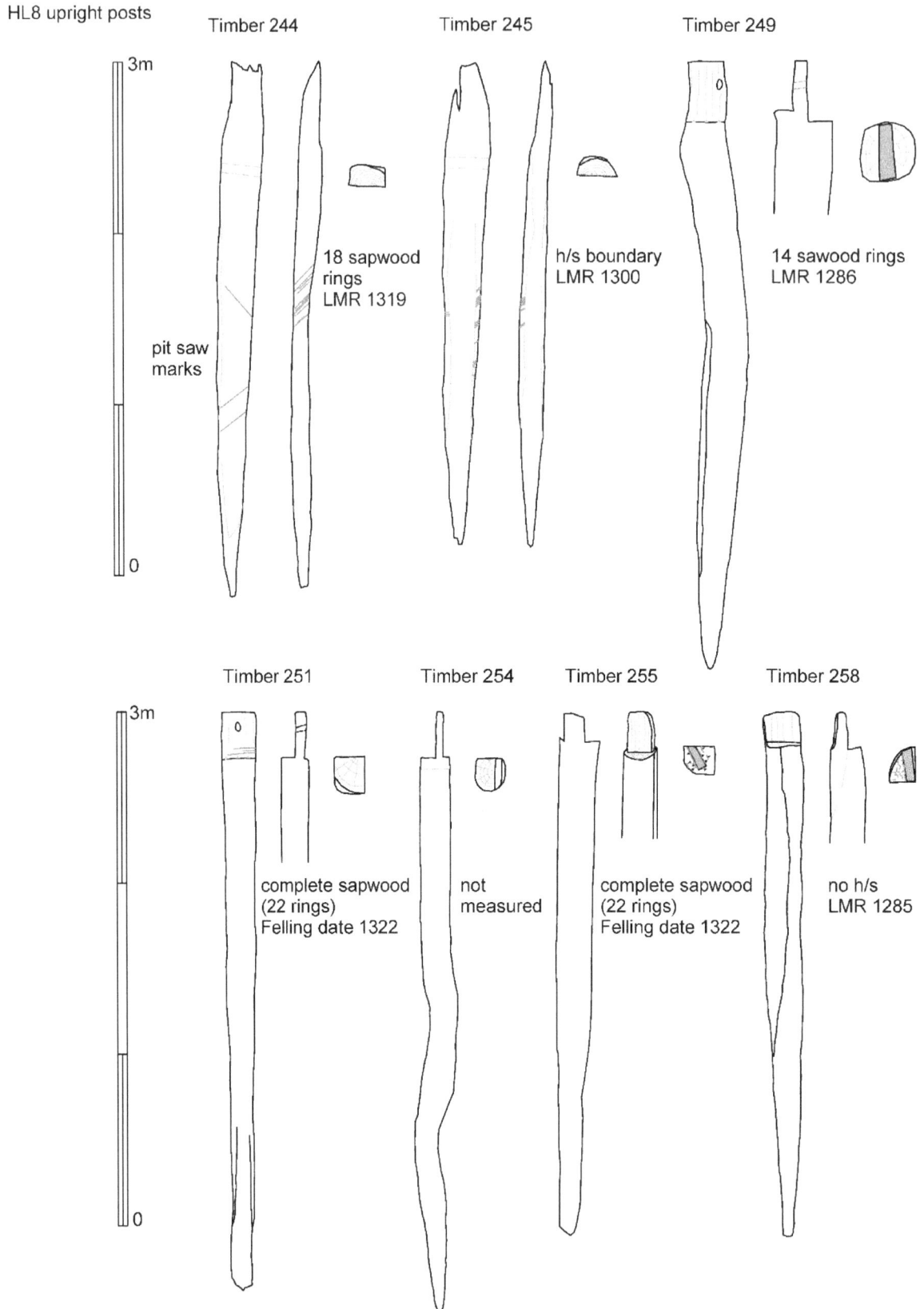

Figure 82: HL8 timbers.

fashioned to wedge the timber against another, as opposed to a premeditated formal joint.

The circuit of pile posts appeared to enclose an area between 10–14m^2: the exact dimensions were difficult to surmise as few of the posts were *in situ*. The structure

was significantly larger than HL6. Within the timber frame masses of roughly hewn sandstone blocks had been dumped, particularly along the upstream western edge (Figure 83, bottom right). The irregularity of the tenons (asymmetrical shoulders, not centred across the timber, dowels that were not centred etc.) suggest that the timbers

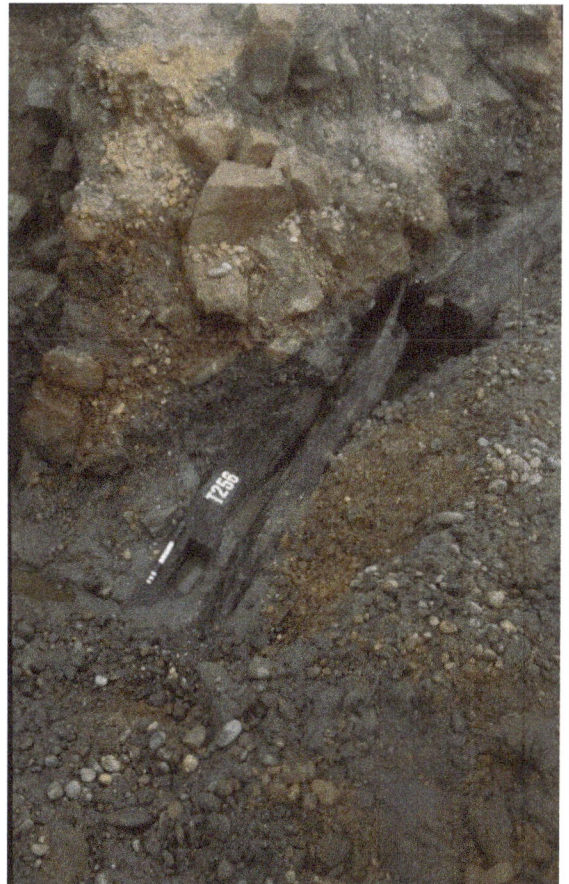

Figure 83: Jetty Structure HL8. Top left: Tenon 249, top right: cut marks on Tenon 258. Left: pre-excavation shot of Jetty Structure HL8 looking north, below: looking west. Bottom left: Part-excavated with Trunk 250 to the left and the upturned Post 249 in the foreground. Bottom right: Timbers 246, 254 and Trunk 253 below *c.* 1.5m of stone infill.

were cut and shaped piecemeal, during construction, rather than pre-fabricated on dry land and reconstructed in the water. Uprights were presumably pile driven into the gravel at distances suitable to the beams selected for the horizontal 'ring beam'. The through mortices on the beams were then presumably prefabricated on land, to a size to accommodate the uprights, and then the tenons were cut into the uprights. Some were then secured with a peg that would have passed through both the ring beam and the tenon, although none of the pegs survived. It appears not to have been considered necessary for the beams to sit squarely on the shoulders of the tenons, although this would have given greater structural stability. The shoulders varied, but were frequently asymmetrical both in area and

height, and often they were not cut flat (Figure 83, top left and right).

Of the 18 recorded timbers sixteen were sampled for dendrochronological dating (Figure 84). Four samples had complete sapwood and felling dates between 1322–1325. A further five samples had either some sap rings or a heartwood /sapwood boundary and extrapolated dates not inconsistent with the complete felling dates (i.e. they could have been felled in the 1320s had they had their full complement of sap rings). Two samples had no heartwood/ sapwood boundary: tenon 258 had a Last Measured Ring of 1285 and could have been felled in the 1320s, Timber 242 was the worn and battered hefty plank with three mortices. It had a Last Measured Ring date of 1239, but a

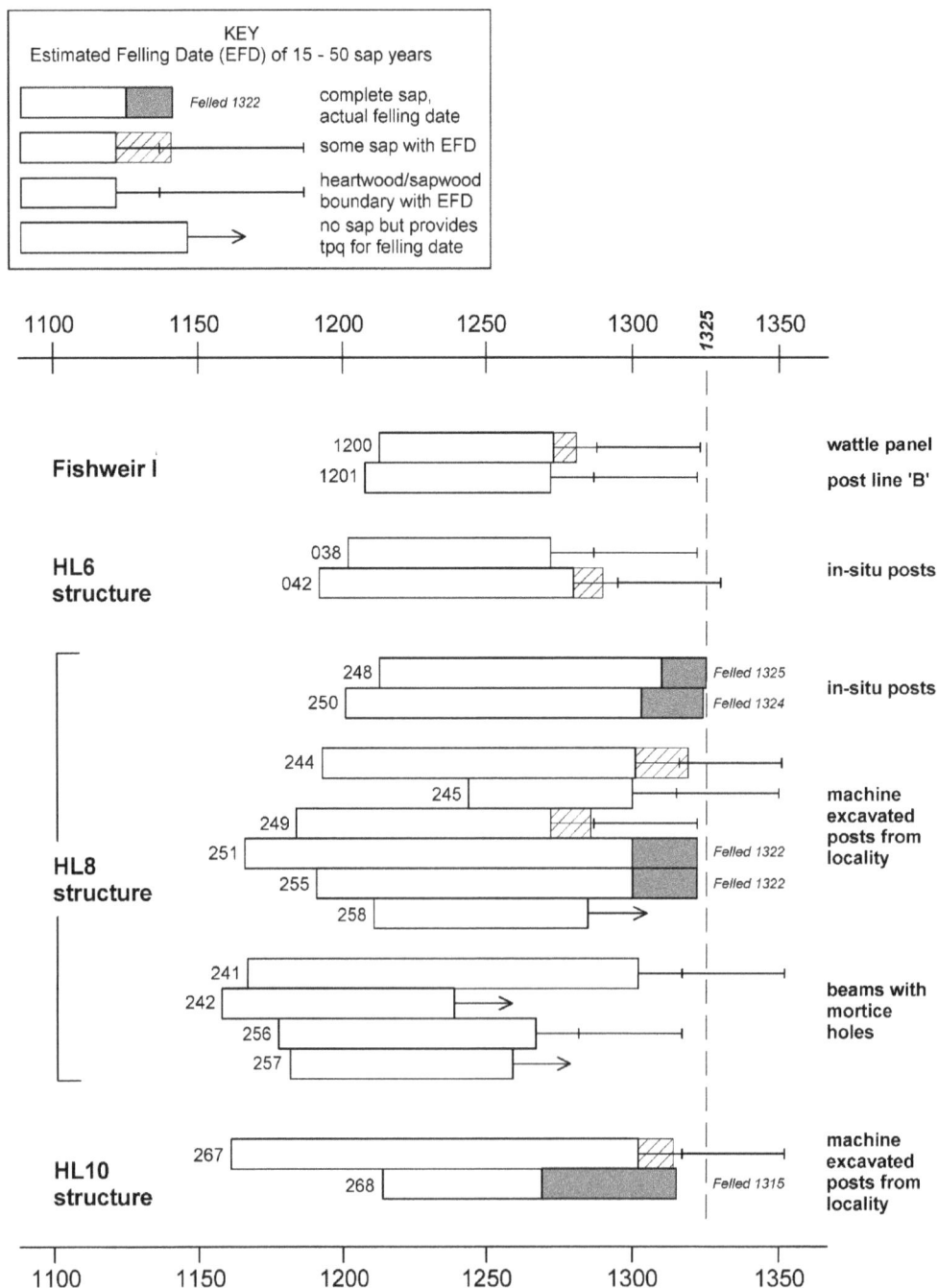

Figure 84: Tree ring dates from the early 14th century jetty structures and Fish weir I.

first Measured Ring roughly comparable to the other dated timbers. Four samples did not date (243, 247, 252 and 254). Therefore all the dated samples were growing concurrently and complete felling dates suggests HL8 was constructed in or soon after 1325. The pit saw marks of timber 244 are, to the authors' knowledge, the earliest record of sawyer technology in the Midlands.

Site HL9

HL9 was an observation of a cluster of stones, revealed during machine quarrying of the river gravels. The cluster was located (Figure 1), but severe machine disturbance meant no further recording was possible. The nature of the sandstone rubble, the approximate size of the cluster and its location (just upstream of HL6) suggests it was also a bank-side structure. It may have once been enclosed in a timber crib that had eroded or might be a simple variation comprising merely dumped stones to act as a bank-side projection into the channel or localised armouring of an eroding bank.

Site HL10

HL10 was also an observation of a cluster of machine-excavated rubble stones. It was located 46m to the west of HL8. Three machine excavated timbers were also associated with the stones: T266, a tapered post with a tenon (quarter convertion, 3.60m long by 220 x 160mm cross-section), T267, a pile post without a tenon (quarter

conversion, 5.57m long by 240 x 220mm cross-section) and T268, a whole trunk with a felling wedge at one end (1.60m long by 220mm diameter). Timber 266 and 268 both had felling dates of 1315 and T267 had a last ring date of 1314 (including 12 sap rings. The site is likely to be the remnant of an eroded jetty.

Site HL11

HL11 was an observation of a cluster of stones, 34m west of HL10, and a similar interpretation to that of HL9 is suggested.

Site HL13

HL13 comprised a cluster of large stones that probably represent a destroyed jetty or crib.

Eastern Extension Phase 5 Structure

Some 27m to the west of Fish weir II the very broken remains of a timber and stone structure were recorded cut into alluvial clay (Figure 1 and Figure 85). The observation was made in the edge of the quarry after the side collapsed following a flooding episode. Three upright timber pile posts were observed, together with at least two courses of stone blocks, apparently behind the timber posts. The posts were sampled for dendrochronological dating and suggest a late 13th century date for the structure (Table

Figure 85: Phase 5 timber and stone structure.

Table 6: Phase 5 timber and stone structure, tree ring dating results

Timber number	Total rings	Sapwood rings	First measured ring date	Last heartwood ring date	Last measured ring date
1200	69	8	1213	1273	1281
1201	65	h/s	1208	1272	1272
1203	72	17	—	—	—

6). It would seem likely that this structure was also a jetty or crib.

Discussion of Jetty Structures

The jetty structures were located along the Castle Donington bank of the Trent for a length of at least 250m. Of the 13 dated samples from the jetties there are no timber dates inconsistent with a post-1325 construction date, and some suggestion (based on three samples) that HL 6 and 10 may have been constructed some 10 years earlier, around 1315. The structures are no longer interpreted as 'shoot' structures, bank-side works to protect an eroding river bank (Cooper and Ripper 2000; 2001; Cooper 2003), but likely to be jetty structures associated with fishing. Similar structures on the rivers Severn and Wye are termed cribs and are used to channel the river in such a way as to create scour pools and fast-running eddies, conditions that would attract salmonid fish.

6

Palaeochannels

Site HL1

HL1 was a deep incised Devensian gravel-filled channel observed at the eastern extent of the quarry and probably represents the sand and gravel bars of the HL3 palaeochannel.

Site HL3

A large 150m length of a silted palaeochannel was observed in the south-east of the quarry. It cut into the remnant of Holme Pierrepoint terrace (HL4 area). The radiocarbon dates (Table 3) puts the channel into the beginning of Younger Dryas Stadial (12,890–11,650 cal BP, following Pettitt and White 2012), or Greenland Stadial 1, the last cold snap prior to the Holocene. The palaeochannel fill of fine varved silts suggests that it represents an avulsed channel. Malcolm Green wood (pers. comm.) reported the presence of cold climate beetles in soil samples. Radiocarbon assay was undertaken on seeds and wood fragments.

Site HL7

A silted palaeochannel observed across the quarry associated with the medieval structures.

Site HL14

The remains of an Iron Age channel system were recorded across a large area divided by an unexcavated bund left to protect a gas main. To the east of the bund the northern edge of a silted palaeochannel was observed briefly before ground works to build up the haulage road obscured the deposits. The gravel suite to the north of this was recorded in section (the northern extent of the pit), showing Mercian mudstone overlain by Holme Pierrepont gravels, in turn overlain by Holocene gravels. The interface between Devensian and Holocene was clearly seen as an unconformity and by the typically different hues to the gravels. An ice wedge also confirmed the interface.

To the west the final channel state, prior to silting, appears to have been bifurcating around a central sand and gravel island. Four bog oak trunks (Timbers 392, 394, 396 and 397), a non-oak stump (T395), a split timber (T391) and small roundwood pieces (T393) were recovered from the base of the anaerobic silts. To the south of the channel was a remnant of the Holme Pierrepont terrace seen previously to the east of Tipnall Bank. An ice wedge was observed in the southern quarry edge, confirming the early date for the terrace. A short length of a north-south ditch was also recorded at the eastern end of the exposed terrace. Although this produced no dating evidence its stratigraphic position, sealed by 1m of alluvium would suggest that it is pre-modern.

HL15: Channel System

Overburden removal revealed a series of east-west linear silt-filled depressions. Within a clay silt channel bordering the northern extent of the quarried area two timbers were recorded: Timber 440 was a large, but partially desiccated oak trunk and Timber 441, a large trunk that had been crosscut. No tool marks survived but both timbers were recorded and sampled for dendrochronological analysis.

Limited gravel extraction towards the south of the stripped area also revealed a cluster of *in situ* piles (young oak and non-oak) seen in a working section. Limited clearance around the pile posts (T442 and T443) located a further post (T445), while erosion of the quarry face revealed another pile (T444) further to the west. The timbers may be part of a fish weir, bank revetment or some other riverine structure.

Table 7: Radiocarbon results from channel HL3 including Cal BP dates

Code	Lab. Number	Radiocarbon Age BP	Calibrated Results BP: (2 sigma, 95% probability)	Calibrated Results BC: (2 sigma, 95% probability)
HL3 base	Beta-157316	11,390 ± 60	Cal BP 12,620–12,980	Cal BC 11,440–11,180
HL3 top	Beta-157317	10,920 ± 80	Cal BP 12,615–12,980 Cal BP 13,010–13,065	Cal BC 11,115–11,065 Cal BC 11,030–10,670

Table 8: Radiocarbon result from channel HL14

Code	Lab. Number	Sample type	Radiocarbon Age BP	Calibrated Results BC: (2 sigma, 95% probability)
HL14	Beta-157318	Thistle seeds>50	2190 ± 40	Cal BC 385–165

7

Discussion and Conclusions

The Hedge Weir Fishery

It has been argued persuasively that fish weir structures of hedge weir type were constructed to procure large catches of silver eels during their autumnal downstream migration (Losco-Bradley and Salisbury 1979; Salisbury 1981). The timing of the migration is controlled by a number of environmental parameters including hydrometric, meteorological and temporal factors (Cullen and McCarthy 2003). Monitoring of the eel fisheries of the River Shannon, Ireland over a two decade period has demonstrated that high channel discharge rates and cooler water temperatures increase the number of silver eels initiating their runs. While these factors partly obscure another underlying temporal factor, the lunar periodicity with increased runs in the fourth quarter of a lunar cycle. The fisheries of the confluence zone of the Middle Trent would have the advantages of the wide catchment area of the Trent basin, including the upland zone to the north. This wide catchment area meant that the Trent has the largest discharge of all British rivers (Brown 2009). Precipitation in the upland zone would have quickly provided the Middle Trent with a large discharge of cool waters thus encouraging large eel runs at predictable times.

From the fisheries mentioned in the Domesday Survey it is obvious that eels were their main catch e.g. at Martley two weirs rendered 2,500 eels and five stitches, an extra 125 eels (Hooke 1985, 131). The renders for the 22 *piscariae* of the Trent mentioned in the Nottinghamshire Domesday are exclusively for eels (Salisbury 1981, 34). Fisheries were often associated with Domesday mills and often the mill's render was expressed in terms of money and eels. Where resort was made to render in kind eels were more frequent than grain or malt or rye (Loyn 1962, 359). As late as the 19th century eels were still caught in substantial numbers at the other Castle Donington fishery at King's Mills (Green 1960).

An ancillary fishing installation at HL5 was the eel trap structure, dating to the 10th century, and thus broadly contemporary with the upstream fish weir. This artificial backwater area was used for catching yellow eels, using two catching methods, small bottle-shaped baskets with non-returnable valves and eel tufts, baited brushwood bundles. A pulse stick head, a plunger used to scare eels into hiding was also found in the same area. Remarkably, a wetland Bronze Age site at Must Quarry Farm in Cambridgeshire has hedge weir type structures, several small yellow eel basket traps and an artefact that looks similar to the pulse stick head (Symonds 2012; M. Beamish pers. comm.).

The Water Mill Fishery

The latest of the wattle and post fish weirs at Hemington Quarry appears to date from the 11th century and probably reflects local and national concerns for the effects on fish stocks and, possibly, navigation. There were great changes in fishing practices along the Trent and the other great British rivers during the medieval period. There were both concerns about the sustainability of fish stocks and the conflicting requirements of navigation (Losco-Bradley and Salisbury 1979). An enactment by Edward the Confessor in 1065 ordered the destruction of fisheries along the four Royal rivers Thames, Trent, Severn and Yorkshire Ouse (Hagen 1992, 163). It would seem that the term fishery referred to the physical barriers such as hedge weirs. The Magna Carta granted salmon rights of protection by an order that 'All fish-weirs shall be removed from the Thames, the Medway, and throughout the whole of England, except on the sea coast.' In 1378 there was a Royal Commission to enquire into the obstructions along the Trent finding that the river was not navigable due to the 'very many wears, mills, dams, pales and kidells' and their removal was ordered (RBN, 199).

The fishing apparatus that is observed in the 12th century are large baskets set on the large stone weir of HL12. It is speculated that the original function of HL12 may have been a mill dam. It is also possible that the weir was purpose-built as a basket weir. The form of the well preserved basket trap is very similar to one described by Tebbutt and Sayce (1936, 129) in a discussion of the different traps used in Lincolnshire: The grig trap, used to catch silver eels, was four feet 10 inches (1.47m) long and made of closely woven split osiers. Within the trap two cones of pointed sticks, chairs, were used as non-return valves. These traps, and the similarly designed net cods, were used for catching silver eels. They were placed, with their entrance upstream, in a gap in the middle of a net, which was stretched across the narrow part of a watercourse. The Lincolnshire traps were not baited though their counterparts in other regions, such as Worcestershire, were. A dog ulna was recovered from the catching chamber of the complete HL12 basket. As silver eels stop eating when migrating such baiting was superfluous (Moriarty 1978). Browning (below) suggests that the bone was merely washed in.

Cribs and Anchor Stones: A Change in Fishing Methods?

The series of jetty structures along the Castle Donington bank of the Old Trent have been dated to the early 14th century. Previous publications (e.g. Cooper 2003) suggested that these bank-side installations might be termed 'shoots' after the Trent watermen vernacular for structures used to protect banks from erosion (Salisbury 1985). However, this is problematic in that there are no associated remains of stone and timber revetments between the structures. It is suggested that these structures were fishing cribs, structures built out from the riverbank to create a turbulence thereby forming a scour pool and a stretch of water with strong eddies. Such conditions encourage the development of fish lies, especially salmon. Cribs are common devices used in salmon fisheries today. While those discussed by Seebohm (1905) were used for net fishing, nowadays, and presumably in the past, they are used by game anglers for producing conditions suitable for fly fishing. There is mention of angling and fly fishing in the 1496 edition of the Book of St. Albans: The treatyse on Fysshinge with an Angle.

Seebohm (1905, 153) suggested that the wattled hedges or hackle-weirs on the river Wye could also be likened to cribs, more permanent structures used to make an eddy in which fish are caught from a boat using a stop-net.

'This mode of fishing is also peculiar to the Wye and Severn. The boat is fixed by two long stakes sideways across the eddy, and a wide net, like a bag with its open end stretched between two poles, is let down so as to offer a wide open mouth to the stream which carries the closed end of the bag-net under the boat. When a salmon strikes the net the open end is raised out of the water, and the fish is taken out behind. This clumsy process of catching salmon is the ancient traditional method used in the Wye and Severn fisheries, and so tenaciously is it adhered to that the fishermen can hardly be induced to substitute more efficient modern improvements.'

Some of the more curious artefacts from Hemington Quarry are the so-called anchor stones, large grooved stones some found with preserved withy ropes. Several of these stones had traces of withy ties surviving in the grooves; these have produced radiocarbon dates from the 8th–9th century to the 13th–14th century (Salisbury and Brown 2009, 12). Salisbury puzzled over these artefacts for many years, wondering if they might be related to fishing with nets either as anchors or counter-weights for lifting nets. Although he had speculated that the stones may have been used as boat anchors (Salisbury1988), when he published his summary of finds from the watching brief of 1985–1994 he was adamant that they were not used as boat anchors (Salisbury and Brown 2009, 12). We would suggest that they should be re-considered in the light of the stop-net fishing methods employed on the Wye and Severn. They may have served as boat anchors allowing similar fishing methods. Perhaps anchor stones were used instead of stakes in stretches of deep pools within the river. Indeed, Salisbury (2009, 12) reported six examples of stones being found in pairs. There is a strong correlation between pools and anchor stones: there is a cluster of over 30 grooved stones in the vicinity of the Bridge III scour pools, with another group immediately downstream from the 12th century mill dam. Radiocarbon dates of the associated

withies suggest a use from the 8–9th to the 13th–14th century, though four out of five were dated to the later period. A further late example is suggested by another anchor stone, a re-used Bridge III ashlar block (Salisbury 1990, 98, illus 15); the bridge's demise is thought to have been in the early 14th century (Cooper 2009).

Locating and Identifying the Fishery

It is possible to place the fishery evidence from Hemington Quarry within an historical framework. Green (1960) has discussed the evidence for two separate fisheries at Castle Donington and suggested that the fisheries described in an 18th century survey can be traced back to the medieval period. One fishery was attached to King's Mills and was associated with the Hospital of St John the Baptist. The other fishery was upstream of King's Mills and was referred to as the Manorial Fishery. A survey of the Melbourne estate in 1846 is recorded in a memo book of the Castle Donington Manor where reference is made to an earlier survey of 1761 where the 'Fishery of the Trent' is described as running from 'King's Mills and ending at the bottom of Donington Meadow called Tipnall.' Tipnall Meadow has been identified as the major land parcel within the Castle Donington block of the Hemington Quarry Western Extension (Cooper *et al.* 1996, 16). A combination of cartographic and documentary evidence allows a correlation between mapped and named land parcels. The Castle Donington Enclosure Map (LRO PP 352) shows three fields in the study area, the two eastern fields owned by Mr Roby Burgin. Cross referencing to a 19th century terrier, Estate at Castle Donington, Carr Samuel (LRO 3D 42/M33/1C), a pre-enclosure map of Hemington of 1740 (LRO Misc 533) and A Plan of an Estate at Castle Donington...the Property of Roby Burgin Esq. of 1809 (LRO 3D 42/M/44) allows the fields to be identified as Tipnall Meadow.

An Inquisition Post Mortem of 1310–11 on the properties of Henry Lacy, Earl of Lincoln shows alongside the watermills (King's Mills) 'a separate fishery worth 1 mark yearly'. The manor passed to his daughter Alice, countess of Salisbury and Lincoln, and wife of Thomas, earl of Lancaster and Leicester (and the Duchy of Lancaster *c.* 1400). An extent of the Manor of Castle Donington of 1326 says 'there are two water mills which are worth yearly with the fishery 100s.' There is also mention of a separate net fishery in the Trent worth 30s. In the Duchy of Lancaster's Minister's Account for 1399 (TNA ref 728–11987) the fisheries were valued separately: King's Mills and fishery were valued at £12. 4s. 4d. while the other fishery was valued at £12. 10s. 0d. The discrepancy between the values at the beginning and end of the 14th century are likely to represent more realistic valuations at a time of economic hardship following the Black Death (Paul Courtney pers. comm.).

In February, 1309 a dispute between Henry Lacy, Earl of Lincoln and owner of the Castle Donington estate and the Abbey of Chester, the owner of the Weston estate, was resolved with the unusual arrangement of the manor of Castle Donington having full access over the fishing rights of the Trent. The later manorial history is well covered in Fisher and Lee (2016). The northern bank remains the county boundary in this reach of the Trent and fishing rights along both banks are with the Derby Railway Angling Club, the present owners of the manorial fishery.

The Wider Context of the Fishery

Despite the existence of prehistoric, Romano-British and early medieval channels at Hemington Quarry there is no evidence for human exploitation. The earliest fish weirs seem to be from the 8th century, but possibly late 7th century if we take the earliest dates in the calibrated radiocarbon dates from HL5. The evidence from the quarry reflects a national pattern of increasing intensity of landscape exploitation: Rippon (2010, 64) has described the late 7th century and the 'long eighth century' as a key formative period in southern England with an increased intensity of landscape exploitation and economic expansion, with concomitant technological changes. During this period there was great investment in methods to increase the economic benefits of rivers including fish weirs and mills. Murphy (2010, 218–219) presents a corpus of dated fish traps from coastal and estuarine fisheries in East Anglia and south-east England. The majority fall between AD 600–900 with an intense phase of activity in the 7th and 8th centuries. He speculates that the decline may be due to:

- Overfishing of the coastal fish stocks
- Social disruption of the ninth century Anglo-Scandinavian conflict
- Development of the deep sea fishing industry

By contrast inland fisheries continue to thrive, being well represented in documentary and, increasingly, through archaeological evidence. At Hemington Quarry there is good evidence for fishing from the 7th to 14th century. The lack of dated structures or artefacts after the 14th century at Hemington Quarry is probably due to the avulsion of the Old Trent to the course, more or less, of the current channel (Brown 2009, 156). Documentary evidence for the later medieval period shows that the Castle Donington Manorial Fishery continued to thrive (Green 1960). Although there is an increasing proportion of marine fish imported into inland towns in the late Anglo-Saxon period, e.g. Leicester, freshwater fish remained a dietary staple (Nicholson 1999). The continuation of inland fisheries in England into the 10th century and later would suggest that the Anglo-Scandinavian conflicts and Norman invasion had little impact.

Conclusions

Long term monitoring of alluvial stripping and mineral extraction at Hemington Quarry has revealed a hidden medieval riverine landscape that had been buried by the migrating river Trent in the dynamic confluence zone with the rivers Derwent and Soar. The range of geoarchaeological evidence (structural, artefactual, ecofactual, sedimentological) allows a consideration of not only the past landscapes but the developing taskscapes of the medieval fishing community (*sensu* Ingold 1993; Van de Noort and O'Sullivan 2006). River fisheries are now recognised as an important archaeological asset and have recently been listed by English Heritage as one of 40 Heritage Assets (Jecock 2011). These once common, economically important sites are well attested in the documentary record but their archaeological remains are extremely rare. This rarity is reflected in the very restricted reading list given in the Heritage Assets guidance document. It is hoped that this report will provide a benchmark for their archaeological discovery and analysis, and demonstrate that river fisheries can have 'direct, physical associations' with other historic features in the landscape such as bridges, water mills, road systems and managed rivers (*contra* Jecock 2011).

Edgeworth (2011, 27) has highlighted the work at Hemington Quarry as an exemplary study in undertaking wetland archaeological fieldwork and attempting to 'reconstruct dynamic, flowing riverscapes' from the evidence retrieved in the former river courses. Perhaps the biggest achievement has been to highlight the Middle Trent in general, and the Hemington reach in particular, as one of England's most significant areas for wetland archaeological potential. It has been recognised as such and is included in List A of Historic England's Exceptional Waterlogged Heritage Inventory (Entry 15: Trent Floodplain from Shardlow to Hemington).

Bibliography

Allen, S. *Swarkestone Quarry, Barrow on Trent, Derbyshire (CPB Area 100), Analysis waterlogged timbers and roundwood for Trent and Peak Archaeological Unit.* York Archaeological Trust Conservation Laboratory Report Number 2007/39, 2007.

Allin, C.E. *The Medieval Leather Industry in Leicester.* Leicestershire Museums, Art Galleries and Records Service Archaeological Report no.3. Leicester: Leicestershire County Council, 1981.

Anderberg, A.-L. *Atlas of Seeds and Small Fruits of Northwest-European Plant Species with Morphological Descriptions (Sweden, Norway, Denmark, East Fennoscandia and Iceland). Part 4. Resedaceae-Umbelliferae.* Stockholm: Swedish Museum of Natural History, 1994.

Astill, G.G. *A Medieval Industrial Complex and its Landscape: The Metalworking, Watermills and Workshops of Bordesley Abbey. Bordesley Abbey III.* York: CBA Research Report 92, 1993.

Behrensmeyer, A., and Hill, A. *Fossils in the making: Vertebrate taphonomy and palaeoecology.* Chicago and London: The University of Chicago Press, 1980.

Berggren, G. *Atlas of Seeds and Small Fruits of Northwest-European Plant Species with Morphological Descriptions (Sweden, Norway, Denmark, East Fennoscandia and Iceland). Part 3. Salicaceae-Cruciferae.* Stockholm: Swedish Museum of Natural History, 1981.

Blinkhorn, P. "The Saxon Pottery." In *Roman and Medieval Occupation in Causeway Lane*, edited by A. Connor and R.J. Buckley, 165. Leicester: Leicester Archaeology Monograph 5, 1999.

Blinkhorn, P. "The Early Anglo-Saxon Pottery." In *The Archaeology of Rutland Water: Excavations at Empingham in the Gwash Valley, Rutland, 1967–73 and 1990*, edited by N. Cooper, 98–104. Leicester: Leicester Archaeology Monograph 6, 2000.

Brown, A.G. *Hemington Quarry Western Extension, Hicklin Land, Castle Donington. Geomorphological Report.* ULAS report 97/47, 1997.

Brown A.G., Ellis, C., Potter H., Salisbury C.R. and Wilby R. "The Geomorphology and Environment of the Hemington Reach." In *The Hemington Bridges: The Excavation of Three Medieval B ridges at Hemington Quarry near Castle Donington, Leicestershire*, edited by S. Ripper, and L.P. Cooper, 142–172. Leicester: Leicester Archaeology Monograph 16, 2009.

Browning, J. "Animal Bone." In *Monument, Memory and Myth: Use and Re-use of Three Bronze Age Round Barrows at Cossington, Leicestershire* edited by J. Thomas, 101–103. Leicester: Leicester Archaeology Monograph 14, 2008.

Cappers, R.T.J., Bekker, R.M. and Jans, J.E.A. *Digital Seed Atlas of the Netherlands. Groningen Archaeological Studies 4.* Eelde: Barkhuis Publishing, 2006.

Clark, H.J.S. "The Salmon Fishery and Weir at Wareham." *Proceedings of the Dorset Natural History and Archaeological Society* 22 (1950), 99–110.

Clay, P.N. *Hemington Quarry Western Extension: A Design Specification for Archaeological Work.* University of Leicester Archaeological Services unpublished report, 1997.

Clay, P.N. and Salisbury, C. "A Norman Mill Dam and other sites at Hemington Fields, Castle Donington, Leicestershire." *Archaeological Journal* 147 (1990), 267–307.

Clay, P. "A Norman mill dam at Hemington Fields, Castle Donington, Leicestershire." In *Archaeology Under Alluvium*, edited by S. Needham and M.G. Macklin. Oxford: Oxbow Books, 1992.

Collcutt, S. *Hemington Quarry Western Extension: Scheme of Archaeological Works.* Oxford Archaeological Associates unpublished report, 1997.

Collcutt, S.N. *Fluvial Evolution of the Trent Valley at the Trent-Derwent Confluence, Derbyshire-Leicestershire.* Oxford Archaeological Associates Limited, 1998.

Cooper, L., Howard, J. and Knight, D. Hemington. *Quarry Extension, Hicklin Land, Castle Donington, Leicestershire: An Archaeological Desk-based Assessment.* Trent and Peak Archaeological Trust 1996.

Cooper L. "Castle Donington/Lockington-Hemington, Hemington Quarry." *Transactions of the Leicestershire Archaeological and Historical Society* 73 (1999), 91–7.

Cooper, L. "Hemington Quarry, Castle Donington, Leicestershire, UK: a decade beneath the alluvium in the confluence zone." In *Alluvial Archaeology in Europe*, edited by A.J. Howard, M.G. Macklin and D.G. Passmore, 27–41. Lisse/Abingdon/Exton (PA)/Tokyo: A. A. Balkema, 2003.

Cooper L. and Ripper, S. "Castle Donington, Hemington Quarry (SK 455 299)." *Transactions of the Leicestershire Archaeological and Historical Society* 74 (2000), 233–5.

Cooper L. and Ripper, S. "Castle Donington, Hemington Quarry (SK 455 299)." *Transactions of the Leicestershire Archaeological and Historical Society* 75 (2001), 137–42.

Coward, J. and Ripper, S. "Castle Donington, Willow Farm (SK 445 288)." *Transactions of the Leicestershire Archaeological and Historical Society* 73 (1999), 87–91.

Cullen, P. and McCarthy, T.K. "Hydrometric and meteorological factors affecting the seaward migration of silver eels (*Anguilla Anguilla*, L.) in the lower River Shannon." *Environmental Biology of Fishes* 67 (2003), 349–357.

Darrah, R. "The Tools and Joint Types used in the construction of the Hemington Bridges." In *The Hemington Bridges: The Excavation of Three Medieval Bridges at Hemington Quarry near Castle Donington, Leicestershire*, edited by S. Ripper, and L.P. Cooper, 2009a. Leicester: Leicestershire Archaeology Monograph 16, 2009, 96–113.

Darrah, R. "Sources and conversion of the trees used in the Hemington Bridges". In *The Hemington Bridges: The excavation of three medieval bridges at Hemington Quarry near Castle Donington, Leicestershire*, edited by S. Ripper, and L.P. Cooper, 2009b. Leicester: Leicestershire Archaeology Monograph 16, 114–139.

Davis, S. "Water-power in medieval Greenwich." *Current Archaeology* 236 (2009), 30–35.

Dyer, C.C. "Gardens and garden produce in the Later Middle Ages." In *Food in Medieval England*, edited by C.M. Woolgar, D. Serjeantson, and T. Waldron, 27–40. Oxford: Oxford University Press, 2006.

Edgeworth, M. *Fluid Pasts: Archaeology of Flow.* London: Bristol Classical Press, 2011.

Elliott, L., and Knight, D. "An early Mesolithic site and first millenium BC settlement and pit alignments at Swarkestone Lowes, Derbyshire." *Derbyshire Archaeological Journal* 119 (1999), 74–153.

Fisher, P.J. and Lee, J.M. *The Victoria History of Leicestershire: Castle Donington.* London: Victoria County History, University of London, 2016.

Fischer, C. "Hulpiberen. *Skalk* 5 (1984), 3–9.

Fraser, F. C. and King, J. E. "Faunal remains." In *Excavations at Star Carr*, edited by J. G. D. Clark, 70–95. Cambridge: Cambridge University Press, 1954.

Green, G. H. *Historical Account of the Ancient Kings Mill (Castle Donington, Leicestershire)*, Castle Donington: Workers' Educational Association, 1960.

Hagen, A. *A Second Handbook of Anglo-Saxon Food and Drink.* Hockwold-cum-Wilton: Anglo-Saxon Books, 1992.

Hamerow, H. *Excavations at Mucking, Volume 2: The Anglo-Saxon Settlement.* London: English Heritage/British Museum Press, 1993.

Harcourt, R. A. "The dog in early historic Britain." *Journal of Archaeological Science* 1 (1974), 151–176.

Hartley, F. *The Medieval Earthworks of North-West Leicestershire.* Leicester: Leicester Museums Publication, 1984.

Higham, N.J. and Ryan, M.J. *Landscape Archaeology of Anglo-Saxon England.* Publications of the Manchester Centre for Anglo-Saxon Studies. Woodbridge: The Boydell Press, 2010.

Hooke, D. *The Anglo-Saxon Landscape: The Kingdom of the Hwicce.* Manchester: Manchester University Press, 1985.

Ingold, T. "The temporality of the landscape." *World Archaeology* 25.2 (1993), 24–174.

Ingrouille, M. *Historical Ecology of the British Flora.* London: Chapman and Hall, 1995.

Jecock, M. *River Fisheries and Coastal Fish Weirs.* Introductions to Heritage Assets: English Heritage, 2011.

Jenkins, J.G., *Nets and Coracles.* London and Vancouver: David and Charles, 1974.

Knight, D., Baker, S., Keech, M., Lewis., MacIntosh, A., Platt, L. and Richards, G. "Swarkestone Quarry, Barrow-Upon-Trent (SK 34652780; SK 34302750)." *Derbyshire Archaeological Journal* 127 (2007), 135–38.

Knight, D. "A regional ceramic sequence: pottery of the first millenium BC between the Humber and the Nene." In *Prehistoric Britain: the Ceramic Basis*, edited by J.D. Hill, and A.Woodward. Oxford: Oxbow Books, 2002.

Legge, A. J. "The aurochs and domestic cattle." In *Extinctions and Invasions: A Social History of British Fauna*, edited by T. O'Connor and N. Sykes, 26–35. Oxford: Windgather Press, 2010.

Legge, A. J. And Rowley-Conwy, P. A. *Star Carr Revisited* London: Birkbeck College, 1988.

Liebermann, F. *Die Gezetze der Angelsachsen, 3 vols.*

Losco-Bradley, P.M. and Salisbury, C.R. "A mediaeval fish weir at Colwick, Nottinghamshire." *Transactions of the Thoroton Society of Nottinghamshire* 83 (1979), 15–22.

Losco-Bradley, P.M. and Salisbury, C.R. "A Saxon and Norman fish weir at Colwick, Nottinghamshire." In *Medieval Fish, Fisheries and Fishponds in England,* edited by M. Aston, BAR British Series 182, 329–51. Oxford: British Archaeological Reports, 1988.

Loyn, H.R. *Anglo-Saxon England and the Norman Conquest.* London: Longman Group Ltd., 1962.

Mitchell, N.C. "The Lower Bann Fisheries." *Ulster Folk Life* 11 (1965), 1–32.

Mockton, A. "Analysis of waterlogged plant macrofossils from Late Neolithic, Bronze Age and Medieval palaeochannels C-F at Hemington Quarry, Leicestershire (A34.1994)." In *Late Glacial, Neolithic, Bronze Age and medieval environments from Hemington Quarry, Castle Donington, Leicestershire*, edited by M Beamish, 21–35. University of Leicester Archaeological Services Report 2002–166, 2002.

Mould, Q., Carlisle, I. and Cameron, E. *Leather and Leatherworking in Anglo-Scandinavian and Medieval York. Archaeology of York The Small Finds 17/16.* York: York Archaeological Trust, 2003.

Moriarty, C. *Eels*. London and Vancouver: David and Charles, 1978.

Murphy, P. "The landscape and economy of the Anglo-Saxon coast: New archaeological evidence." In *Landscape Archaeology of Anglo-Saxon England*, edited by N.J. Higham and M.J. Ryan, 211–222. Publications of the Manchester Centre for Anglo-Saxon Studies. Woodbridge: The Boydell Press, 2010.

Mynard, D. "Some weights from the Rivers Great Ouse, Ouzel, Nene and Tove." *Records of Buckinghamshire* 21 (1979), 11–29.

Needham, S., and Macklin, M. G. *Archaeology Under Alluvium.* Oxford: Oxbow Books, 1992.

Nicholson, R. "The fish remains." In *Roman and Medieval Occupation in Causeway Lane, Leicester*, edited by A. Connor and R. Buckley, 333–337. Leicester: Leicester Archaeology Monographs No. 5, 1999.

O'Sullivan, A. "Place, memory and identity among estuarine fishing communities: interpreting the archaeology of early medieval fish weirs." *World Archaeology* Vol 35.3 (2003), 449–68.

Pettitt, P. & White, M. *The British Palaeolithic: Human Societies at the Edge of the Pleistocene World.* London and New York: Routledge, 2012.

Rackham, O. *Trees and Woodland in the British Landscape: The Complete History of Britain's Trees, Woods and Hedgerows.* London: Phoenix Press, 2001.

Rahtz, P. and Meeson, R. *An Anglo-Saxon Watermill at Tamworth.* CBA Research Report 83. London: Council for British Archaeology, 1992.

Rayner, T. *Archaeological Watching Brief on the Route of the A6 Alvaston Bypass, Derbyshire.* Report No.38/04 Archaeological Project Services, 2004.

RBN *Records of the Borough of Nottingham Vol I,* 1155–1399. London: Bernard Quaritch & Thomas Forman and Sons, 1882.

Reimer, P.J., Baillie, M.G.L., Bard, E., Bayliss, A., Beck, J.W., Blackwell, P.G., Bronk Ramsey, C., Buck, C.E., Burr, G.S., Edwards, R.L., Friedrich, M., Grootes, P.M., Guilderson, T.P., Hajdas, I., Heaton, T.J., Hogg, A.G., Hughen, K.A., Kaiser, K.F., Kromer, B., McCormac, F.G., Manning, S.W., Reimer, R.W., Richards, D.A., Southon, J.R., Talamo, S., Turney, C.S.M., Van der Plicht, J. and Weyhenmeyer, C.E. INTCAL09 and MARINE09 radiocarbon age calibration curves, 0–50,000 years cal BP. *Radiocarbon* 51.4 (2009), 1111–50.

Ripper, S. and Cooper, L.P. *Excavations of a Riverine Landscape at Hemington Quarry Western Extension (Hicklin Land), Hemington Quarry, Castle Donington, Leicestershire (NGR SK 45 29): Assessment Report and Updated Project Design.* University of Leicester Archaeological Services Report 2002–202, 2002.

Ripper, S. and Cooper, L.P. *The Hemington Bridges: The Excavation of Three Medieval Bridges at Hemington Quarry near Castle Donington, Leicestershire.* Leicester: Leicester Archaeology Monograph 16, 2009.

Ripper, S. and Darrah, R., Bridge I: the late 11th to early 12th–century bridge. In *The Hemington Bridges: The Excavation of Three Medieval Bridges at Hemington Quarry near Castle Donington, Leicestershire,* edited by S. Ripper, and L.P. Cooper, 13–43. Leicester: Leicester Archaeology Monograph 16, 2009.

Ripper, S., Coward J. and Clay, P. "Down by the River: Bronze Age and Anglo-Saxon Occupation at Willow Farm, Castle Donington." *Transactions of the Leicestershire Archaeological and Historical Society* 91 (2017), 1–43.

Rippon, S. "Landscape change during the 'long eighth century' in Southern England." In *Landscape Archaeology of Anglo-Saxon England,* edited by N.J. Higham and M.J. Ryan, 39–64. Publications of the Manchester Centre for Anglo-Saxon Studies. The Boydell Press, Woodbridge, 2010.

Salisbury, C.R. "An Anglo-Saxon Fish-Weir at Colwick, Nottinghamshire." *Transactions of the Thoroton Society* 85 (1981), 26–35.

Salisbury, C.R. "Taming the Trent." *East Midlands Archaeology* 1 (1985), 5–12.

Salisbury, C.R. "A watching brief at Hemington Fields, Castle Donington (SK 457 301)." *Transactions of the Leicestershire Archaeological and Historical Society* 62 (1988), 74–76.

Salisbury, C.R. A watching brief at Hemington Fields, Castle Donington (SK 461 307). *Transactions of the Leicestershire Archaeological and Historical Society* 64 (1990), 97–99.

Salisbury, C.R. "Primitive British fish weirs." In *Waterfront Archaeology, Proceedings of the Third International Conference 1988,* edited by G.L. Good, R.H. Jones, and M.W. Ponsford, 76–87, CBA Research Report 74. London: Council for British Archaeology. 1991a.

Salisbury, C.R. "A possible 13th century bridge over the Trent at Hemington Fields, Castle Donington (SK 4595 3024)." *Transactions Leicestershire Archaeological and Historical Society* 65 (1991b), 96–7.

Salisbury, C.R. "The archaeological evidence for palaeochannels in the Trent valley." In *Archaeology Under Alluvium,* edited by S. Needham and M. G. Macklin, 155–162. Oxford: Oxbow Book, 1992.

Salisbury, C.R. "An early 12th century mill float and more news of the Norman Bridge at Hemington Fields, Castle Donington (SK 4595 3024)." *Transactions Leicestershire Archaeological and Historical Society* 67 (1993), 73–6.

Salisbury, C.R. "Hemington Fields, Castle Donington (SK 4595 3024)." *Transactions Leicestershire Archaeological and Historical Society* 68 (1994), 179–82.

Salisbury, C.R. and Brown, A.G. 2009. "The archaeological background." In *The Excavation of Three Medieval Bridges at Hemington Quarry near Castle Donington, Leicestershire,* edited by S. Ripper, and L.P. Cooper, 7–12. Leicester: Leicester Archaeology Monograph 16, 2009.

Shwarze, F.W.M.R. "Wood decay at the Microscope." *Fungal Biology Reviews* 21 (2007), 133–170.

Schweingruber, F.W. *Microscopic Wood Anatomy.* Zug, Switzerland: Ed Zürcher, 1982.

Sinha, V.R.P. and Jones, J.W. *The European freshwater eel.* Liverpool: Liverpool University Press, 1975.

Stace C. *New Flora of the British Isles.* Cambridge: Cambridge University Press, 1997.

Symonds, M. "Waterworld: Must Farm's Bronze Age boats." *Current Archaeology* 623 (2012), 12–19.

Syson, L. *British Water-mills.* London: B.T. Batsford Ltd., 1965.

Tabor, R. *The Encyclopaedia of Green Wood Working.* Eco-Logic Books, 2000.

Tebbutt, C.F. and Sayce, R.U. "Fenland eel-traps." *Man* 36 (1936), 129–179.

Tesch, F.-W. *The Eel.* London: Chapman and Hall, 1977.

Van de Noort, R. and O'Sullivan, A. *Rethinking Wetland Archaeology.* London: Duckworth, 2006.

Vøllestadt, L.A., Jonsson, B., Hvidsten, B.A., Naesji, T.F., Haraldstad, O. and Rudd-Hansen, J. "Environmental factors regulating the seaward migration of European silver eels." *Canadian Journal of Fish and Aquatic Science* 43 (1986), 1909–1916.

Von Brandt, A. *Fishcatching Methods of the World.* Farnham, Surrey: Fishing News Books, 1984.

Von Den Driesch, A. *A Guide to the Measurement of Animal Bones from Archaeological Sites.* Cambridge, Massachusetts: Peabody Museum of Archaeology and Ethnology, Bulletin no. 1, 1976.

Williams, D.F and Vince, A.G. "The characterization and interpretation of early to Middle Saxon Granitic Tempered Pottery in England." *Medieval.Archaeology* 41 (1997), 214–220.

Appendix I

Mill Paddles

Matthew Beamish

In the Hemington Reach, a 2km stretch of the River Trent encompassing the Hicklin Land excavations, the 12th century mill dam at Hemington Fields (Clay and Salisbury 1990) and the Hemington Bridges (Ripper and Cooper 2009), seven mill paddles have been recovered. While none of the mill paddles can be directly associated with either of the proposed mill sites (the Stone Weir HL12 and the Hemington Fields mill) their proximity suggests they are likely to have derived from these locations. Although no part of any water mill wheel was found there is compelling evidence that river mills were located at both sites; monumental timbers associated with both weir sites suggests large scale water management, numerous fragments of mill-stones and mill-stone rough-outs were found around both weirs and at Pontylue Quarry (previous name for Hemington Quarry) part of a timber wheel-breast was located in the watching brief following the mill dam excavation (Clay and Salisbury 1990). The seven paddles provide an invaluable diagnostic element that can suggest both the mechanism for how a watermill functioned and indicate the variability of medieval milling technology.

Four of the mill paddles (A313.1993: T640, T641, T671 and T705) were located during excavation of the medieval river gravels both up and downstream of Hemington Bridge I (Ripper and Cooper 2009). The remaining three (A53.1985: T223, T262 and T268) were found during the watching brief by C.R. Salisbury and Burleigh Archaeological Fieldwork Group, two of which have been reported on previously (Salisbury 1993, 73–76). All were downstream of the Hicklin Land weir.

The Hemington paddles were all basically flat wooden boards. All paddles had peg holes, suggesting they were attached to the wheel via a central batten. Some of the paddles had fragments of battens (here, "staves") attached with pegs through holes bored through the centre of the assembly. Some of the paddles also had rectangular slots, near each end. These are interpreted as housings for braces between adjacent paddles (here "stabilising struts").

To ease description, the paddles are referred to as having top edges (the edge furthest from the wheel); and where apparent, top sides (the side to which the stave was fixed). When viewed top face and top edge up, the paddle has a left and a right.

Of the seven examples, five are very similar and look to be derived from the same type of single rim wheel, although with some variability in dimensions. The remaining two share some characteristics but are not clearly related. The

larger of the two was probably from a double rimmed wheel of a size not inconsistent with the wheel breasting found in 1985 (Clay and Salisbury 1990, 287).

Similarity of Paddles

All the paddles were made from high quality straight grained knot-free oak. Both radial and tangential conversions are evident. All the paddles were notably thin boards, varying between 10 and 20mm. Paddle lengths are reconstructed where possible (Table 9). It has been assumed that for a single rimmed wheel the supporting stave would have been central: an un-central stave would result in a paddle prone to twist, damage bearings, waste energy, and transmit power unevenly.

Width of paddles are more difficult to assess; the thinness of the boards and the very straight grained timber selected for their manufacture, combined with an eroding use and disuse environment has resulted in loss of material and breakage along the grain with no clear indications of such damage remaining visible.

Re-use of materials for the paddles cannot be discounted as two paddles (T640 and T 671) have dowel holes that do not obviously function in the proposed reconstruction (Figure 86). However, a water-wheel was an expensive assembly, manufactured by skilled wood wrights. In addition to the structural form of the wheel and the gearings involved, the paddles were specialised pieces, of little width compared to their large surface area (presumably to minimise weight) and selection of the right timber for the job was imperative.

The paddles have been placed in four wheel types; the first two (Types 1a and 1b) are typologically similar single rimmed wheels of two sizes, with single stave fixed paddles, with stabilising struts. The third (Type 2) is probably a single rimmed wheel with identical stave fixed paddles to Type 1 (with possibly two or more boards per paddle) but no stabilising struts. The fourth (Type 3) is from an extremely wide double rimmed wheel.

Dating

Four of the paddles were found in gravels post-dating the construction of Bridge I (AD 1111): T640, 641, 671, 705) and probably date from at least before the mid-13th century. T262 was found in the north of the quarry pit (Figure 86), 390m NNE from Bridge I. It has a dendrochronological last measured heartwood ring of AD 1061, so a late 11th – early 12th century date can be assumed. T268 was found 230m

Table 9: Hemington mill paddles 1985–1993

Timber no.	Length	Reconstrctd Length	Width	Depth	Stave w x d	Stave pegs dia	Peg centres	Lath slots	Strut to stave pegs (centres)	Strut to top edge	Other pegs dia A313.1993	Grid Ref	Comments
Type 1A: Single rim, with stabilising strut holes, 690–750mm wide													
223	365	700	240 ?Complete	15>	-	18?	-	74 x 20		22			
268	625	690	150 Incomplete	10	-	24?	-	70 x 30	265	50			
705	750	750	240	20	60 x 35	20*	120	65 x 20<25 70 x 15+	270 240	27 40		171.10/563.2026.24m AOD	* 1 peg wedged & mushroomed 70 x 15 + 240; 40
Type 1B: Single rim, with laths. 870mm wide													
262	850	870	270 Complete	20>	-	25?	70	72 x 24	275	37			? x24 360 67R
641	794	870	180	15>	55 x 30	19 Rwood pegs	70	58 x 30 ? x35	360 290	40 40		169.80/564.40 25.97m AOD	?broad axe marks on paddle/ 22mm blade marks by slot
Type 2 Single rim, ?multiple boards, no laths, 800mm min													
640	780	780+	180	15>	-	20/21	90	None but dowel holes in place 20 25	270 300		12, with rw peg, poss related to stave repair ?12, at end	161/568 26.70m AOD (approx)	
Type 3 Double rim, no laths, 1300mm min													
671	1100	1300 ?	265	20		22	140	None	None	-	25;40 *	163/579 25.23m AOD	

All dimensions in mm.
* Repairs.

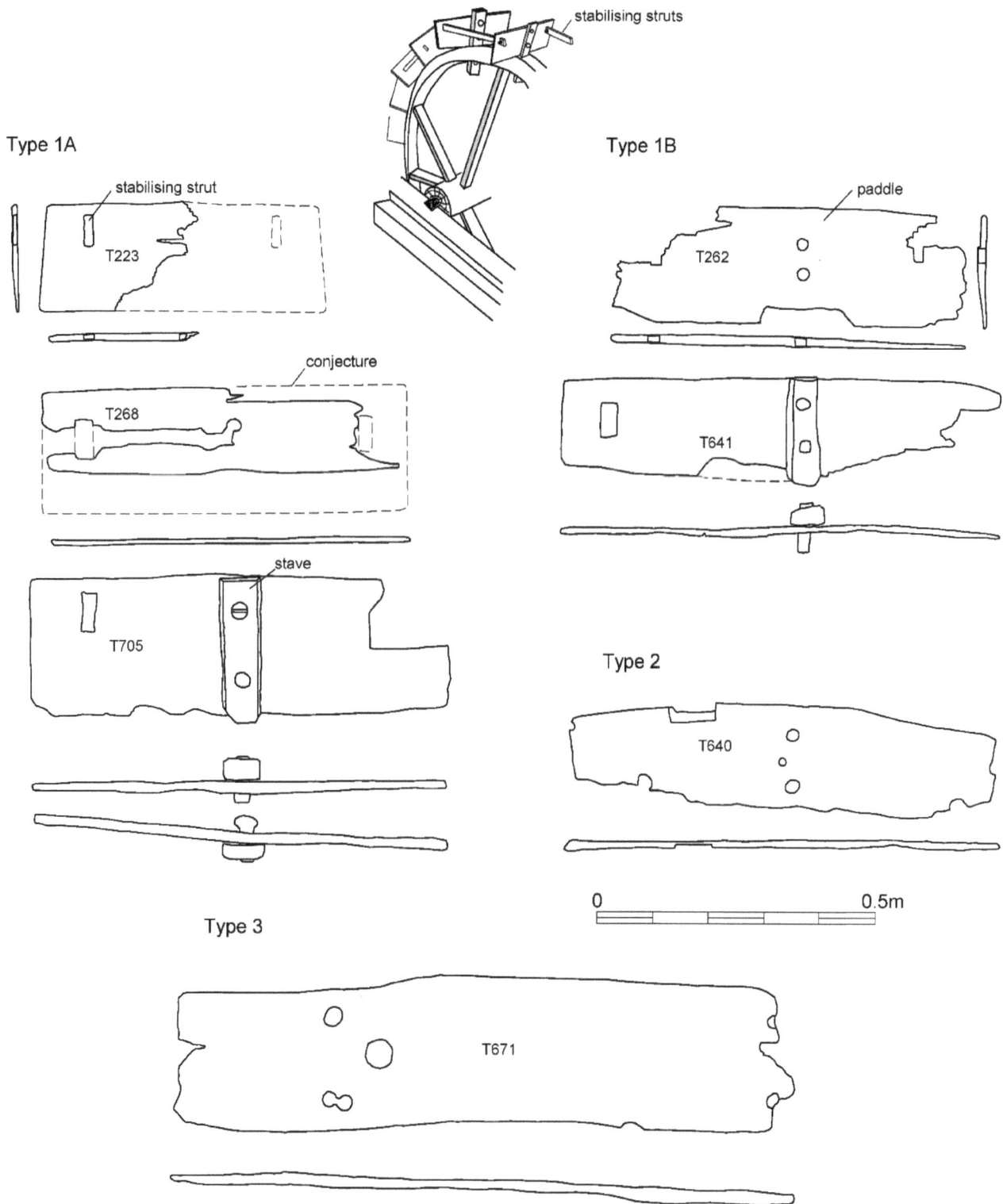

Figure 86: Mill paddles from the Hemington Reach.

northeast from the late 11th century bridge in the vicinity of a fish weir (CRS PL48) and T223 was found some 200m due East of the 12th century mill site (CRS PL9).

Type 1a (Timbers 223, 268, 705)

The reconstructed lengths vary between 690mm (T223) and 750mm (T705). This is an 8% variation in length that may have significance if the paddles all originated from the same wheel. T223 and T705 are of identical width

(240mm); and both are considered complete. T268 has clearly been damaged.

Stave and Stave Fixings

Only T705 has a remnant of its stave surviving. The stave is of roughly squared heartwood with a rectangular section at the finished end (72mm x 23mm), squarer at the broken end (63mm x 35mm). The staves' fixing pegs are at 120mm apart (centre to centre); the stave fixings of

T268 must be at least 90mm apart and T223 more than 70mm apart.

T705 had two heartwood section pegs in a 20mm diameter holes. One of the pegs had had a wedge driven centrally into its end, slightly proud of the stave surface. The same pegs head was distinctly "mushroomed". The pegs protruded between 15mm and 25mm from the paddle.

Peg hole diameter was not independently recorded for either T223 or T268. From the drawn record, the surviving hole on T223 is 18mm, and T268, 24mm.

Slots for Stabilising Struts

The slots for stabilising struts fall within 65–74mm long and 15–30mm wide. The slots' centres are set at either 240mm or 270mm from the projected centre of the paddles; the top of the slots vary between 22mm and 50mm from the top edge of the paddle.

One corner of the left-hand slot on T705 was distinctly rounded. If this were caused by boring the corner of the housing, the bore diameter would only be 5mm, although it is conceivable that the roundness was caused by wear.

Type 1b (Timbers 262, 641)

The reconstructed length of both paddles is 870mm. T262 is 270mm wide and looks mostly complete. T641 is clearly broken along its lower edge, as is the stave. T262 has a small fracture on its lower edge probably caused by pressure from the stave.

This fracture has previously been interpreted as 'a small recess for the felloe' (Salisbury 1992, 74). However, there is no positive evidence for a joint; apart from the top side being along the grain and therefore straight edged, the ends of the recess are irregular. Similar fractures were noted on other pieces of oak during recording, (for example T640); this type of fracture is characteristic of the drying of waterlogged wood. Salisbury's reconstruction must therefore be questioned on the evidence for setting the paddles into the felloe, rather than at a certain distance from it.

Stave

The stave survives partially on T641, and similarly to T705, it is of roughly squared heartwood, and wider at its broken end (60mm x 30mm) than at its finished end (50mm x 25mm). The upper edges of the stave have been finished bevelled.

Fixings

The stave on T641 is secured with two roundwood pegs in 19mm diameter holes. The peg protruded up to 30mm from the paddle on one side and was just proud of the stave.

Peg-hole diameters were not accurately recorded for T262; from the drawn record the hole diameter is around 25mm.

Slots for Stabilising Struts

The slots vary between 58–72mm long and 24–35mm wide. The slots are at either 275–290mm or 360mm from the centre of the paddle. The tops of three slots are between 37–40mm from the top edge, and one is perhaps over 60mm (reconstructed).

The Type 1 Slots for Stabilising Struts

Three paddles have all or part of two slots preserved. In each case the slots are not symmetrical with the stave, but offset by 30mm (T705) (closer on right-side), 75mm (T641) (closer on right-side) and 85mm (T262) (side not evident). This lack of symmetry may suggest the paddles did not come from the same wheel but it is also possible that the pattern was intentional. To allow the stabilising strut to pass through the paddle would allow a more secure pegged fixing (see sketch reconstruction on Figure 86).

Salisbury has reconstructed a wheel based on T262 (Salisbury 1993, 76). His drawing shows the stabilising struts scarfed together in the slots, held together by wedges, (which is based on the combination of evidence from medieval Danish mills (Fischer 1984, 6) and the 12th–14th century mill at Bordesley (Astill 1993, 218, fig 94). If this was the method used on the Type 1 paddles, the wheel would have been out-of-balance, unless the off-centre laths were acting as a counterbalance for some other feature for which there is no evidence. The Bordesley paddle has symmetrical lath slots (Astill 1993, 218, fig 94). The laths on the Type 1 Hemington paddles were alternatively face joined between each paddle, with the slot positions alternating between adjacent paddles.

Type 2 (Timber 640)

Although the surviving evidence from this board is incomplete and it is possible that this was not a wheel paddle at all, some interpretations can be made confidently.

The grain of the board is less straight than for the other pieces, and of not such high quality. However, the board may have been chosen for this characteristic. The board has an overall convex plan shape. One edge surprisingly retained a small amount of sapwood. The ends of the piece do not survive cleanly, but both are perpendicular to the convex top edge. The clearly broken dowel at one end is mirrored by damage at the other end that could conceivably have been caused by a shearing peg.

The length of this board is difficult to reconstruct exactly but is likely to be not much more than 780mm. The board's width may have been nearer 190mm, assuming that the mid-point between the peg holes was the centre of the board (which is broadly so for the other examples).

The fixing holes (20–21mm diameter) for the central stave are 90mm apart (centre to centre) and not dissimilar to the Type 1 paddles. There are no stabilising strut slots as such, but there are dowel peg holes (20–25mm diameter) that could have fixed additional staves to the board, or battens, securing this board to other boards. There is also a small hole (12mm) just off-centre from the stave hole which is not interpretable.

A vertical undershot wheel, with no bracing laths and with three boards per paddle is illustrated by Fischer (1984, 6).

Type 3 (Paddle 671)

The length of this board is again difficult to reconstruct, but must exceed 1300mm (if the peg holes were symmetrical). There are no fixing holes for a central stave, but there are symmetrical pairs of fixing points (22mm apart), suggesting staves at each end. One of these holes has been re-bored with a slightly larger bit (25mm as opposed to 22mm). Alternatively, the holes could have fixed two battens, butting this board to another which itself be connected to the wheel with a single stave.

Given the width of the board, a considerable degree of support would have been needed for such a paddle as it has no supporting struts (unless the Type 1 paddles are considerably over-engineered). Two staves may have provided this strength.

It was suggested that that the wheel breasting (T178) found in 1985 accommodated a 1.20m wide wheel (Clay and Salisbury 1990, 287); the breasting is 1270mm internal width from the published drawing. The breasting was in fragmentary condition when recorded, and may have shrunk slightly prior to recording. It is not implausible that the paddle (at 1300mm width) and the breasting came from the same construction.

This interpretation augments Clay's contention (1990, 287–8) that the Hemington Fields wheel breast supported a double rimmed single wheel.

Appendix II

Pottery and Ceramic Building Material

The Prehistoric Pottery (Patrick Marsden)

The excavations produced 69 sherds of prehistoric pottery weighing 345g. On the basis of fabric and wall-thickness a general date of late Bronze Age or Iron Age is suggested. The lack of scoring may perhaps suggest a late Bronze Age or early Iron Age date. However, the pottery sample is small and may represent plain vessels from within the East Midlands scored ware repertoire and be of a middle or late Iron Age date.

The igneous rocks present in the vessel in fabric R1 are probably of a Charnwood granodiorite type. Iron Age pottery containing similar inclusions has been found at Swarkestone Lowes, Derbyshire (Elliott and Knight 1999). Several rim sherds are present with a flattened lip, pinched out externally.

The Roman Pottery (Patrick Marsden)

Two sherds of probable Roman grey ware weighing 8g were recovered from Trench 56, but are unstratified.

Catalogue of medieval and post-medieval pottery (Deborah Sawday)

Context/SF	Sherd No.	Weight (g)	Comment
247	1	5	Fabric SP2 Nottingham splashed ware, 12th century
Trench 1, Topsoil	2	30	Fabric EA7 Slipware, 18th century.
Trench 2, Topsoil	1	30	Fabric EA6 Blackware, 18th century. ?Chamber pot.
Total	**4**	**65**	

The Early Anglo-Saxon Pottery (Nicholas J Cooper)

Three sherds of hand made pottery of Early Anglo-Saxon date (*c.* AD 450–650), weighing 20g, have been identified and catalogued below. All three sherds conform to the range of clay fabrics expected from material of this date from the city and county (Blinkhorn 1999, 165; Blinkhorn 2000). The fabric series established for the material from Causeway Lane, Leicester is used here (Blinkhorn 1999).

The clay fabrics are diagnostically prepared using crushed or weathered rock fragments as opening materials. The use of granite (particularly Mountsorrel Granodiorite) from the Charnwood area of NW Leicestershire (fabrics 4 and 6) is now widely recognised across the Midlands (Williams and Vince 1997), as well as sandstone perhaps from the Nottinghamshire or Derbyshire areas (Sherwood and Millstone grits respectively). This issue of sourcing is poorly understood at present.

Table 10: Prehistoric pottery from feature south of Tipnall Bank

Context/SF	Location	Sherd No.	Weight (g)	Fabric	Comments
5	Trench 22	1	3	R1	
120 [cut 121]	HL4, pit fill	59	290	R1	Same vessel with rim sherds present
120 [cut 121]	HL4, pit fill	1	5	Q4	
122 [cut 123]	HL4, pit fill	2	36	Q4	
204		5	5	Q4	
SF1, 120, [cut 121]	HL4, pit fill	1	9	Q5	
Total		**9**	**348**		

Fabric codes (ULAS fabric series 15.07.02): R1, igneous rock inclusions, probably granodiorite; Q4, sandy ware with quartzite inclusions; Q5, quartzite inclusions.

Catalogue of ceramic building materials

Context/ SF	Frag No.	Weight (g)	Comments
Trench 1 US	1	110	Possibly land drain, modern
Trench 1 US	2	30	Modern
Trench 2 US	1	30	Modern
Total	**4**	**170**	

Catalogue of fired/burnt clay materials

Context/ SF	Frag No.	Weight (g)	Comments
122	34	327	Possibly burnt daub
130	3	6	
Total	**37**	**333**	

Appendix III

Animal Bones

Jennifer Browning

A small collection of animal bones were retrieved during the work at Hicklin Land, Hemington, Leicestershire in 1998. Due to the nature of the archaeology, several of the bones were recovered from contexts that were neither discrete nor securely-dated and are likely to have been re-deposited by fluvial activity. However, some are of intrinsic interest such as an aurochs bone recovered from silted gravels of the river channel.

The bones were examined with reference to skeletal material held by the School of Archaeology and Ancient History, University of Leicester. Observations were recorded on a *pro forma* spreadsheet. Species, bone element, side and completeness were recorded and the bones were examined for the presence of butchery marks, gnawing and other modifications. Where possible, measurements have been taken following von den Driesch (1976).

Results and Discussion

A total of 16 bones were recovered during hand-excavation (Table 11 and Figure 87). Although environmental samples were taken for sieving, no bones were retrieved during this work.

Domestic species are most common in the assemblage, with wild animals represented by aurochs, red deer and goose (which could be wild or domestic). The preservation of the bones was variable, with some specimens in good condition, retaining their cortical surfaces, while others had an abraded appearance with porous and flaking surfaces.

The aurochs bone was in particularly poor preservation, brittle with a flaking cortex. It therefore seems likely that the bones were subjected to different taphononic processes.

The aurochs tibia was recovered from silting in the gravels. Aurochs bones have been recovered from other Leicestershire sites, primarily quarries, such as Cossington (Browning 2008) and Watermead Country Park, Birstall (Gouldwell n.d.). The aurochs is considered to be a grazer predominantly, like its domestic descendants (cattle) and is therefore associated with open grassland, although would also be likely to utilise woodland (Legge 2010, 28). Aurochs were very large mammals with heights of approximately 1.5m for females and 1.8m for males (ibid). The largest assemblage currently known in Britain was discovered at Star Carr, Yorkshire, initially reported upon by Fraser and King (1954) and later reconsidered by Legge and Rowley-Conwy (1988). The aurochs appears to have become extinct during the Bronze Age in Britain, mainly as a result of habitat reduction caused by land clearances and exacerbated by infectious diseases (Legge 2010, 34).

It was possible to take a series of measurements from the Hicklin Land aurochs tibia, shown in Table 2. Comparative measurements from the distal tibiae at Star Carr range from 73.1 to 88.2mm (Bd) and 53.0–63.3mm (Legge and Rowley-Conwy 1988, 131, Table 8). The Bd (width) of the Hicklin Land tibia is well within the Star Carr range but the Dd (depth) is greater than the examples in the Star Carr assemblage. No comparative greatest length (GL) or proximal measurements were available.

Table 11: Animal bones recovered from the site

SF/Context	No. of Bones	Location	Brief Description
c.328	3	Silt layer at north end of weir, in the apex of the V (section 30.3)	pig tibia; goose tibio-tarsus; large mammal cervical vertebra
c.366	1	-	cattle mandible fragment
SF48	1	Towards north end of weir. Plan 37.1	sheep skull
SF50	1	Sample 107. Inside 1st basket of eel trap SF50. May be further bones from this context (see Anita)	dog ulna
u/s	5	'Over shoes' at north end of weir	horse scapula; horse radius (juvenile); deer antler; domestic fowl humerus; large mammal thoracic vertebra
u/s	4	North end of weir	sheep/goat metacarpal; horse mandible; large mammal thoracic vertebrae
u/s	1	XA23.1998 From gravels (an area quarried between the bridges and Hicklin Land. Near x2 V-shaped fish weirs, but these are medieval in date	aurochs tibia

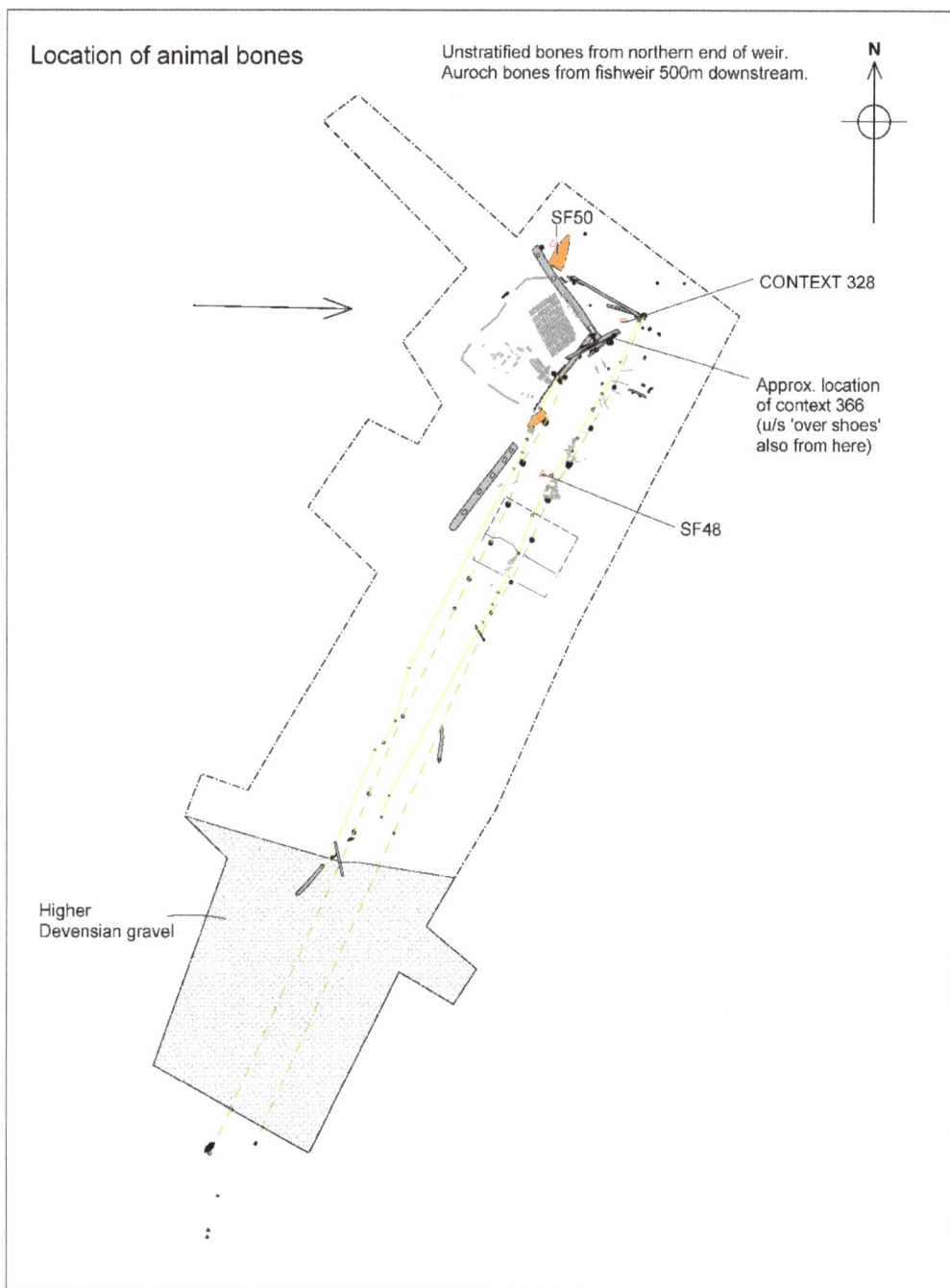

Figure 87: Location of animal bones from the stone weir, HL12.

Table 12: Measurements referred to in the text

Cntxt	Bone	Spcies	GL	Bp	SD	Bd	Dd	Shoulder height	Comments
u/s	tibia	aurochs	463	117.8	55.9	79.5	65.7	No calculation available	Fresh break but poss. to reassemble and measure
S107	ulna	dog	160					(2.78*GL)+6.21=451mm*	

*Calculation after Harcourt (1974).

The bone recovered from the eel basket (SF50) was identified as a complete and well-preserved dog ulna, which produced an estimated shoulder height of 0.45m (Table 2), using Harcourt's (1974) calculation. There were no visible butchery marks. The presence of the ulna in the eel basket is surprising, as part of a dog foreleg would be an unusual form of bait. The dog is not usually a food animal and it may make more sense to bait the trap with more readily available butchered stock animals or, more likely, fish. When fleshed, the ulna is paired with the radius and the absence of this bone may also suggest that the bone was washed in, rather than deliberately deposited.

The silt layer at the top of the weir (context 328) produced evidence for pig, goose and a large mammal vertebra, while a fragment from a cattle mandible was recovered from another stratified context (366).

The unstratified material included several horse bones, among which was a radius from a foal; a shed antler of red deer; a sheep/goat metacarpal, while the bird bones were of goose and domestic fowl. The variation in the condition of the bones suggests that they are likely to have different provenances. It is not possible to establish where the animals might have entered the water; however, fluvial processes are likely to scatter even whole carcasses. The rate at which the connective tissue weakens varies for different parts of the anatomy (heads are often lost first) and bone elements are likely to travel through the water at variable rates (Behrensmeyer and Hill 1980, 170–81). Therefore the bones may have been deposited as the result of successive fluvial episodes.

Appendix IV

Analysis of Waterlogged Wood and Plant Macrofossils from the Anglo-Saxon and Medieval Fish Weirs

Part I: Wood Analysis of the Fish Weirs and Eel Basket (Anita Radini)

Material and Methods

The sampling of wood was conducted on site by cutting a portion of the posts, rods, sails and brushwood. Withies used for the eel basket were also sampled. The wood was then labelled, bagged and kept in water in a dark and cool environment to preserve the waterlogged remains. Wood posts/piles were selected and identified for radiocarbon analysis, and they have been discussed elsewhere in this report.

Wood Analysed for this Report

Wood used for the construction of five structures was analysed for this report (see Table 2: wood catalogue):

1. Fish weir HL5, hurdle structure II, dating between the 9th and 10th century AD: wood posts and one rod
2. HL5, eel weir, dating between the 9th and the 10th century : wood posts and wattle panels
3. HL12, stone weir, dating the 12th century AD: posts, hurdle, wattle panel (rods and brush wood) and rod and brushwood from eel basket
4. HL15, dating the 9th–10th century AD: loose post
5. Fish weir II, dating between the 9th and the 10th century AD: rods

Identification and Nomenclature

The identification of the wood was conducted using thin sections of the wood, cut with a sharp razor, and observing them under a microscope with magnification range between 40x to 200x. Identification keys and reference collection were also consulted.

Many species of wood do not have anatomical features that allow precise identification; for example, oak (*Quercus* spp.), willow (*Salix* spp.), poplar (*Populus* spp.) and birch (*Betula* spp.). In the same way, it is not always possible to distinguish between willow and poplar, both are in fact part of the same family (*Salicaceae*) and have similar anatomical characteristics. The identification between willows and poplars is based on the differences existing between rays, which are not always clearly visible in tangential sections (Schweingruber 1982). When the differences in the rays were not visible or well preserved, the wood has been described as willow/poplar (*Salix/Populus*).

Nomenclature adopted for this report is shown below:

Corylus avellana L.	Hazel
Fraxinus excelsior L.	Ash
Quercus spp.	Oak
Salix spp.	Willow
Populus spp.	Poplar
Salix/Populus	Willow/Poplar
Betula spp.	Birch

Annual Ring Counts and Analysis

The species analysed for these report belonged to tree species that have wood growing in annual increments, and with distinctive characteristics of wood produced in specific seasons, such as summer or winter for example (Schweingruber 1982). Therefore it was possible to estimate the age of the wood at the moment of cutting and in several cases it was also possible to establish a cutting season.

Recording

The wood analysed was recorded providing brief description of the wood, identification, annual rings count, diameter of the wood, cutting season wherever possible and evidence of tool mark, if visible. In some cases the bark and sapwood were missing or too damaged to identify cutting season. The data obtained during the analysis are presented in a wood catalogue (Table 2) and the recording follows that adopted by Allen (2007), in order to allow future comparison between these assemblages.

Results of the Analysis and Discussion

A total of 173 specimens of wood were examined for identification and analysis for this report. About 25% of the wood was sampled from posts/piles, the rest of the specimens came from the lighter structures of the fish weirs and were represented by rods, sails and brush wood. Results are described and discussed below and all presented in Table 2.

Preservation of the Wood

The state of preservation of the wood was found to be from fair to very poor, and evidence of damage to the internal structure of the wood was found in many specimens. The poor preservation encountered was caused by a combination

Table 13: Wood catalogue

Wood Id No.	Structure	Species	Notes (average length of analysed wood: 5cm)	Ring Count and Details
T2	Hurdle Str.II, post	*Quercus* spp.	roundwood, 23cm in diameter, hardwood, extensive sapwood and small fragments of bark	*c.* 35 annual rings, summer cut
T3	Hurdle Str.II, post	*Quercus* spp.	roundwood, 21cm in diameter, hardwood, sapwood and small fragments of bark found in area	*c.* 47 annual ring, winter cut
T4	Hurdle Str.II, post	*Quercus* spp.	roundwood, 20cm in diameter, hardwood, sapwood and small fragments of bark found in area	*c.* 22 annual rings, winter cut
T6	Hurdle Str.II, post	*Quercus* spp.	roundwood, 23cm in diameter, hardwood, decayed sapwood, no bark	*c.* 25 annual ring, late spring/summer cut
T8	Hurdle Str.II, rod	*Betula* sp.	roundwood, 8cm in diameter, high decay, eccentric wood pith	*c.* 14 annual rings visible, outer rings too damaged to establish cutting season
T23	Hurdle Str.II, post	*Quercus* spp.	roundwood, 23cm in diameter, hardwood, sapwood and small fragments of bark found in an area	*c.* 25 annual ring, winter cut
T56	HL5, eel trap structure post	*Quercus* spp.	roundwood, 15cm in diameter, hardwood, sapwood and small fragments of bark, high level of decay in the outer rings	*c.* 28 annual rings, outer rings too damaged to establish cutting season
T59	HL5, eel trap structure post	*Quercus* spp.	roundwood, 13cm in diameter, hardwood, sapwood and small fragments of bark	*c.* 21 annual rings, winter cut
T63	HL5, eel trap structure post	*Quercus* spp.	roundwood, 20cm in diameter, hardwood, no sapwood	*c.* 45 annual rings, outer rings too decayed to establish cutting season
T64	HL5, eel trap structure post	*Quercus* spp.	roundwood, 10cm in diameter, hardwood, sapwood and small fragments of bark found in area	*c.* 27 annual, rings summer cut
T65	HL5, eel trap structure post	*Fraxinus excelsior* L.	roundwood, 23cm in diameter, hardwood, sapwood and small fragments of bark found in area	*c.* 23 annual rings visible, outer rings too damaged to establish cutting season
T71	HL5, eel trap structure post	*Quercus* spp.	roundwood,15cm in diameter, hardwood, sapwood, high fungal decay present	*c.* 28 annual rings, probably winter cut
T79	HL5, eel trap structure post	*Quercus* spp.	roundwood,13cm in diameter, hardwood, sapwood and bark	*c.* 25 annual rings, winter cut
T80	HL5, eel trap structure post	*Quercus* spp.	roundwood,15cm in diameter, hardwood, no sapwood	*c.* 24 annual rings, outer rings too decayed to establish cutting season
T81	HL5, eel trap structure post	*Quercus* spp.	roundwood, 11cm in diameter, hardwood, sapwood and small fragments of bark found in area	*c.* 16 annual rings, summer cut
T85	HL5, eel trap structure post	*Quercus* spp.	roundwood, 23cm in diameter, hardwood, sapwood mostly lost to fungal decay, eccentric wood pith	*c.* 45 annual rings, outer rings too decayed to establish cutting season
T86	HL5, eel trap structure post	*Quercus* spp.	roundwood, 23cm in diameter, hardwood, sapwood loss	*c.* 34 annual rings, outer rings too decayed to establish cutting season
T97	HL5, eel trap structure post	*Quercus* spp.	roundwood, 17cm in diameter, hardwood, sapwood and small fragments of bark found in area	*c.* 27 annual rings, probably winter cut
T308	HL12, post	*Fraxinus excelsior* L.	roundwood, 23cm in diameter, high decayed, eccentric pith	*c.* 34 annual rings, rings very damaged
T329	HL12, post	*Quercus* spp.	roundwood, 22 cm in diameter, high level of decay in the hardwood, sapwood absent	*c.* 25 annual rings visible, very damaged wood
T335	HL12, post	*Corylus avellana* L.	roundwood, 23cm in diameter, hardwood, sapwood and small fragments of bark found in an area	*c.* 25 annual rings, late spring/summer cut
T336	HL12, post	*Quercus* spp.	roundwood, 23cm in diameter, hardwood, sapwood and small fragments of bark found in area	*c.* 32 annual rings late spring/summer cuts

Table 13 *continued*

Wood Id No.	Structure	Species	Notes (average length of analysed wood: 5cm)	Ring Count and Details
T349	HL12, post	*Quercus* spp.	roundwood, 24cm in diameter, hardwood, sapwood and small fragments of bark found in area	*c.* 32 annual rings, winter cut
T354	HL12, post	*Fraxinus excelsior* L.	roundwood, 21cm in diameter, hardwood, no sapwood due to decay	*c.* 43 annual rings, outer rings too decayed to establish cutting season
T355	HL12, post	*Quercus* spp.	roundwood, 25cm in diameter, hardwood, sapwood and small fragments of bark found in area but very damaged by acidity and fungal decay	*c.* 34 annual rings, outer rings too decayed to establish cutting season
T360	HL12, post	*Quercus* spp.	roundwood, 21cm in diameter, hardwood, sapwood and small fragments of bark found in area	*c.* 25 annual rings, late spring/summer cut
T366	HL12, post	*Quercus* spp.	roundwood, 23cm in diameter, hardwood, sapwood and small fragments of bark found in area	*c.* 25 annual rings, winter cut
T367	HL12, post	*Quercus* spp.	roundwood, 22cm in diameter, hardwood, sapwood and small fragments of bark found in area	*c.* 27 annual rings, winter cut
T369	HL12, post	*Quercus* spp.	roundwood, 23cm in diameter, hardwood, sapwood and small fragments of bark found in area	*c.* 32 annual rings, winter cut
T370	HL12, post	*Quercus* spp.	roundwood, 24cm in diameter, hardwood, sapwood and small fragments of bark found in area	*c.* 35 annual rings, summer cut
T371	HL12, post	*Corylus avellana* L.	roundwood, 22cm in diameter, hardwood, sapwood and small fragments of bark found in area	*c.* 28 annual rings, winter cut
T374	HL12, post	*Fraxinus excelsior* L.	roundwood, 23cm in diameter, hardwood, sapwood and small fragments of bark found in area	*c.* 26 annual rings, winter cut
T379	HL12, post	*Quercus* spp.	roundwood, 24cm in diameter, hardwood, some sapwood and small fragments of bark but high decay	*c.* 32 annual rings, outer rings too decayed to establish cutting season
T380	HL12, post	*Salix* spp.	roundwood, 25cm in diameter, hardwood, decayed sapwood, evidence of one lateral branch been trimmed	*c.* 45 annual rings, outer rings too decayed to establish cutting season
T382	HL12, post	*Quercus* spp.	roundwood, 23cm in diameter	*c.* 25 annual rings
T383	HL12, post	*Quercus* spp.	roundwood, 21cm in diameter, hardwood, sapwood and small fragments of bark found in area, eccentric pith, one lateral branch was trimmed	*c.* 44 annual rings, winter cut
T398	HL12, post	*Quercus* spp.	roundwood, 23cm in diameter, hardwood, sapwood and small fragments of bark found in area	*c.* 28 annual rings, winter cut
T441	HL15, loose timber	*Quercus* spp.	roundwood, 20cm in diameter, hardwood, sapwood and small fragments of bark found in area, eccentric pith	*c.* 27 annual rings, late spring/summer cut
T429	HL12, Hurdle 376, Sample 101	*Quercus* spp.	rod, s shaped, possible evidence of coppicing, 4cm in diameter	*c.* 10 annual ring, winter cut
T430	HL12, Hurdle 376, Sample 101	*Corylus avellana* L.	rod, pointed end, bark present, 3.5cm in diameter	*c.* 7 annual rings, winter cut
T431	HL12, Hurdle 376, Sample 101	*Quercus* spp.	rod, no bark, 5cm diameter, pointed end	*c.* 9 annual rings
T432	HL12, Hurdle 376, Sample 101	*Quercus* spp.	rod, bark, 5cm in diameter	*c.* 10, annual rings, winter cut

Table 13 *continued*

Wood Id No.	Structure	Species	Notes (average length of analysed wood: 5cm)	Ring Count and Details
T433	HL12, Hurdle 376, Sample 101	*Salix* sp. L.	rod, pointed end, bark present 3cm in diameter	*c.* 7 annual rings, winter cut
T435	HL12, Hurdle 376, Sample 101	*Quercus* spp.	rod, young wood, no bark 4cm in diameter	*c.* 8 annual rings, late spring/ summer cut
T436	HL12, Hurdle 376, Sample 101	*Corylus avellana* L.	rod, young wood, no bark 5cm in diameter, pointed end	*c.* 12 annual rings, probably winter cut
T437	HL12, Hurdle 376, Sample 101	*Corylus avellana* L.	rod, bark in fragments, damage due to acidity and fungal decay, 5cm in diameter	*c.* 9 annual rings
T438	HL12, Hurdle 376, Sample 101, Panel 210	*Salix* sp. L.	18 rods, bark 3cm in diameter	*c.* 5 to 7 annual rings, winter and summer cut where visible
T444	HL15, upright	*Quercus* spp.	round wood, no bark between 5 cm in diameter	*c.* 8 annual rings
P22	HL5 Hurdle Structure II Panel 22	*Salix* spp., *Quercus* spp. and *Salix/ Populus*, oak	12 rods of different species 3 to 4cm in diameter, mainly willow, and 11 sails A-K, very similar (4 specimens were oak, and two specimens could not be identified as willow due to decay and mechanical damage)	*c.* 7 to 9 annual rings, possibly winter cut, but decay made difficult the study of the rings
P261	HL5, Hurdle Structure I	*Salix* spp.	Sail A-I: 9 rods, 1 ash young wood, 4cm in diameter, the rest is hazel, same profile for diameter and age	*c.* 6 annual rings, cutting season uncertain, some winter some late spring/ summer cut
P240	HL5, Panel 241	*Corylus avellana* L.	28 sails, between 4 to 5cm in diameter	*c.* 7–9 annual rings, probably winter cut
T1159	Fish weir II	*Salix* spp.	8 samples of small rods, *c.* 3cm in diameter, bark still present pointed end visible in some specimens, badly damaged by abrasion and decay	*c.* 5 annual rings visible, but highly damaged by fungal decay
P210	HL12, Hurdle 376, Sample 101	*Corylus avellana* L.	3 rods, around 4.5cm in diameter,, bark still present and pointed ends resulting from 5 vertical cuts, all hazel	*c.* 8 to 10 annual rings, probably winter cut
S66	HL5, eel weir	*Salix/Populus* ssp.	wood brush bundle 35 'twigs', 1.5–2cm in diameter, highly decayed	*c.* 3–4 annual rings, but badly preserved

of natural fungal decay and soil acidity (due to high level of iron found in the depositional environment).

Several fungal spores and hyphae were in fact observed in wood sections during the process of identification in almost all samples. It is possible that fungal decay had already begun before the wood was placed in water, as fungal decay is a process that also affects living wood (Schwarze 2007). However, considering that all the wood analysed shows at least some damage due to fungal decay, it is likely that the process started and spread once the wood was in water and possibly continued during storage at ULAS. It is unlikely that standing trees affected by rot would be chosen for the building purposes, due to the higher chances 'of mechanical failure' in wood affected by fungal decay (Shwarze 2007).

The samples were also found to be 'corroded' and presented iron panels and iron deposits inside the wood cells. This not only reduced the possibility of identification of some specimens, because it altered the appearance of anatomical characteristics of the wood itself, but also caused the softening of the wood, making it very difficult and time consuming when preparing sections required for the identification to species/genus level.

It was noticed that oak wood showed less damage by the acidic environment then other wood specimens. This may be due to the natural acidity of oak wood itself, which possibly increased the survival of oak specimens in an acidic environment.

It is important to note that the wood appeared to be 'swollen' due to the long amount of time spent in water. This may have altered the original diameter of the rods and sail, which mainly consisted of young wood. Hard wood showed less swelling.

General Composition of the Assemblage

Looking at the wood catalogue compiled for this report (Table 2), it is very evident that the difference in species and age is found to correspond with the size and uses of the wood within similar structures.

Posts/Piles: The round wood analysed from all the fish weirs that was used for posts/piles mainly consisted of oak, with fewer specimens being of hazel, ash, and willow. The number of annual rings encountered varied widely among specimens, with anything between 14 and 47 annual rings. The size of the posts/piles was more uniform, suggesting that the wood was deliberately chosen with a preferred 'average' diameter around 200–230 mm, though cases are present in which the posts were between 110 to 150 mm in diameter. Moreover, considering posts within the same 'diameter' and species, the assemblage shows a variety of ring numbers. This fact points to a variety of woodland types being used, some possibly from open woodland with a faster and uniform growth, while other specimens from more close woodland, with eccentric wood piths and irregular growth pattern, being found with slower rate of growth visible in annual rings.

In general the wood identified had evidence of bark left on the wood, where the bark was not visible it is possible that it was not preserved due to the acidity. This suggests the wood was cut and used straight away, reducing the time necessary for the construction of the fishing structures. Only short lengths of wood were available for the analysis so did not show cut marks in most cases, though the few cut marks seen had a sharp edge and were of a pointed shape. It was also noticed, in a small number of cases, that lateral branches were cut off to make the post smoother. The wood seemed to have been cut mainly in winter, with occasional summer and late/spring summer cuts also present. The presence of the bark suggests the work done on the roundwood was kept to a minimal effort, as also suggested by Allen (2007).

Wattle Panels and Brush Wood

The species composition changed when the wood was used to make the woven structures in the fish weirs and the eel basket. In these cases the wood was mainly hazel and willow, with only few pieces of oak. Again, where visible, the most common cutting season was winter. Rods had bark still present and some of them had pointed ends.

It is therefore possible that the choice of wood was due to the different sizes and different strengths required in different parts of the fish weir:

1. oak was more often chosen for the supporting elements
2. willow and hazel, rods and twigs, were used wherever flexibility was needed, in wattle rods and sails for example, as well as in the eel basket and brush wood.

It was found that there was a preferred choice of hazel where rods needed to be over 4cm in diameter while willow was the most common choice for wood below 4cm.

Seasonality

The following considerations can be made regarding the seasonality of construction and use of the fish weirs.

Looking at table 2, it is clear that, among the specimens of wood where the cutting season was visible, the most represented cutting season was winter, in both post/piles and the wood use for lighter structures such as wattle sails and brushwood. Specimens of wood of late spring/summer cuts were also recovered in different elements of the fish weirs as well.

The species of trees represented in the wood assemblage belong to deciduous trees, therefore winter would have made the best time to fell the wood, when most of the leaves had fallen and the sap had gone down. Moreover, late autumn and winter are usually the coppicing seasons for willows and hazel. Cutting a large part of the required wood in winter would allow time to prepare most of the posts/pile, wattles and any other lighter component of the fish weirs, ready for use and repairs.

The presence of wood cut in late spring/summer suggests that during summer construction work on the fish weirs would still be carried out. Summer would also be the best season for this type of work as the level of the river would probably be lower. It is likely that the fish weirs were used to capture silver eels, therefore they were meant to be functional in the autumn season (Cooper and Ripper, this report).

Therefore the cutting seasons represented in the wood assemblage point to autumn being the most likely season of use for the fish weirs, when they would have need to be fully functional for the catching of silver eels on their downstream migration.

Evidence of Coppicing

The archaeological evidence for coppicing is represented by a curve found at the base of the stems. This curve forms while the stems are growing out of the coppice stool and then up towards the light (Rackham 2001).

Despite most of the wood found in the assemblage being from tree and shrub species widely used in Britain for coppicing (hazel, willow, ash and oak) (Rackham 2001), it was not possible to identify coppicing except in one example where the 'S' shaped stem of oak was recovered (T429, HL12, hurdle 376). However, the growth habit and similar patterns in age and size encountered in wood samples from the wattle panels of HL5 and HL12, strongly suggest that both hazel and willow rods were coppiced.

Brief Comparison with Similar Structures

There are other two fish weirs available for comparison found in the River Trent, one at Swarkestone Quarry, Barrow upon Trent in Derbyshire and the other at Colwick in Nottinghamshire, which were respectively analysed by Allen (2007) and Losco-Bradley and Salisbury (1988, cited in Allen 2007). The composition of the species from Hemington Quarry and the fish weir at Swarkestone Quarry are very similar, with the only difference being that birch was recovered among the species found at Hicklin Land and was not found at the other fish weirs. The two structures seem very similar in composition of species and their uses: the choice of hazel and willow for the panels and mainly oak for the posts.

As pointed out by Allen (2007), the wood from the fish weir in Colwick, is different from Swarkestone Quarry, and therefore from Hemington Quarry. Holly (*Ilex aquifolium* L.) was the most common wood used at Colwick with oak and some hawthorn (*Prunus* spp.) represented less. Neither Holly nor hawthorn were found at Hicklin Land. This suggested that similar species were used in Leicestershire and Derbyshire possibly because of the similarity of the environment.

Part II: The Environmental Samples (Anita Radini with Angela Monckton)

Materials and Methods

Six bulk samples were taken to recover any surviving fish bones and paleoenvironmental evidence (see table 1). A sub-sample of one kilogram of each of the six samples was used to process for waterlogged plant remains by wet sieving in a fine sieve with 0.2mm mesh. The whole residue was examined with a stereo microscope at magnification x20 to x40, for plant remains which were removed to glass specimen tubes. Morphological criteria were used for the identification of plant species, based on modern reference material and seed identification manuals (e.g. Berggren 1981; Anderberg 1994; Cappers *et al.* 2006). Plant names follow Stace (1997). The abundance (1 = scarce <10; 2 = moderate 10–50; 3 = frequent >50) of each archaeobotanical type was estimated on the basis of the minimum number of characteristic plant parts. The rest of the bulk samples were sieved and the residues scanned in their entirety for the presence of fish remains.

Charcoal fragments, beetle remains and fly puparia were also noted, estimating their abundance, but these were not removed from the flots. Plant names follow Stace (1997) and remains are all described as waterlogged seeds unless specified otherwise. The plants were tabulated in their most usual modern habitats, based on Ingrouille (1995), to allow future comparison (Table 3).

Results and Discussion

Fish Bones

The analysis was negative for fish bones. None were retrieved in any of the samples analysed; this was probably due to the very high acidity of the soil.

Plant Remains

The analysis produced a variety of waterlogged plant remains, which all showed some damage due again to the acidity of the samples. Most of the plant remains were recovered in a waterlogged state of preservation, though a few charred remains were also found.

The type of remains was very similar in all the samples, with the main difference being in the concentration of remains. The sample found to have the highest concentration of remains was sample from inside the eel basket (sample 65).

A variety of wild species were present in the assemblage from different type of habitat.

Many species indicative of nitrogen-rich habitats, represented by docks (*Rumex* spp.), nettles (*Urtica dioica*), and goosefoot seeds (*Chenopodium* spp.) all commonly found on waste ground and/or cultivated plots. Other plants found on disturbed ground were chickweed (*Stellaria media*), and silverweed (*Potentilla anserina*), the latter a plant of waysides and sandy soils.

A number of plants usually found in grassland pasture were also recovered. These were hawkbit (*Leontodon* sp.), sowthistle (*Sonchus* spp), buttercups (*Ranunculus* sp.) and thistles (*Cirsium* sp.) together with grasses (*Poaceae*), and nettles (*Urtica dioica*) which also grow on pasture.

Aquatic plants which grow in calm or slow-flowing waters were recovered in high numbers, among these particularly

Table 14: Weight and location of the environmental samples

Fish Weir	Sample	Context	Weight (kg)	Sample from inside Eel Basket SF41
HL12	65	336	10kg	Sample from inside Eel Basket SF41
HL12	100	375	10kg	Eel Basket SF50. Sample from between inner and outer basket
HL12	102		30kg	Eel Basket SF50
HL12	103		20kg	Mouth of Eel Basket SF50
HL12	104		20kg	Bottom of outer Eel Basket SF50
HL12	105		20kg	Bottom of outer Eel Basket SF50

Table 15: Waterlogged plant macrofossils from HL12 eel basket

Samples	Sample Number						Common Name
	65	100	102	103	104	105	
Charred plant remains							
Triticum aestivum/durum	1	1	1	1	1	1	Bread wheat grains
Triticum spp.	1	-	-	-	-	1	Wheat grains
Hourdeum vulgare L.	1	1	-	-	1	-	Barley grains
Quercus sp., wood	1	1	1	1	1	1	Oak wood
Charcoal flecks	1	1	1	1	2	1	Charcoal flecks
Aquatic							
Ranunculus subgen. *Batrachium*	3	3	3	1	2	2	Crowfoot
Potamogeton sp.	2	1	2	1	2	1	Pondweed
Marsh or wetland							
Juncus sp	2	2	3	-	1	2	Rushes
Schoenoplectus sp.	1	1	2	1	1	1	Club-rush
Eleocharis palustris L.	3	2	1	1	2	1	Spike-rush
Waterside							
Ranunculus sceleratus L.	1	1	1	1	2	-	Celery-leaved buttercup
Wood or scrub							
Corylus avellana L. nutshell fragments	1	1	-	-	2	2	Hazel
Rubus fruticosus agg.	2	2	2	1	-	1	Bramble
Other plants							
Ranunculus subgen *Ranunculus*	3	1	1	1	1	1	Buttercup
Urtica dioica L.	3	1	1	1	2	-	Nettle
Chenopodium sp.	1	1	1	2	1	2	Goosefoot
Montia fontana L.	1	1	1	1	-	-	Blinks
Stellaria media L.	2	1	1	-	-	1	Chick-weed
Stellaria sp.	2	2	2	1	1	1	Chickweed type
Cerastium sp.	1	1	1	-	-	-	Mouse-ears
Spergula arvensis L.	1	1	-	1	2	-	Corn spurrey
Persicaria sp	-	1	1	-	-	1	Persicaria
Rumex acetosella L.	2	1	2	1	1	-	Water dock
Rumex sp.	2	1	1	1	1	1	Docks
Brassica sp.	1	2	2	1	-	2	Cabbages/mustards
Potentilla anserina L.	2	-	1	-	-	-	Silverweed
Prunella vulgaris L.	1	-	-	-	1	-	Self-heal
Aethusa cynapium L.	1	-	-	-	-	-	Fool's parsley
Cirsium sp.	2	1	-	1	1	-	Thistles
Leontodon sp	2	1	1	1	1	-	Hawk-bit
Sonchus asper (L.) Hill	2	-	-	1	-	1	Prickly sow-thistle
Carex spp.	2	1	3	2	1	-	Sedge
Poaceae	1	-	-	1	1	2	Grasses
Leaf fragments, dicot.	1	-	1	-	-	1	Leaf
Insects remains (beetle thorax)	1	1	1	1	-	-	Beetle thorax
Weight analysed in kilograms	1	1	1	1	1	1	

abundant were: pondweed (*Potamogeton* sp), and crowfoot (*Ranunculus* subgen. *Batrachium*) which has floating leaves.

While plants such as club-rush (*Schoenoplectus* sp.), together with rushes (*Juncus* sp), spike rush (*Eleocharis palustris*) and sedges (*Carex* spp) are commonly found at watersides.

Seeds of water-blinks (*Montia fontana*), were also present and they are normally found in wet ground.

Wood or scrub was represented in some of the samples but in low number. Woody plants included hazel (*Corylus avellana*), and bramble (*Rubus fruticosus* agg.).

Small numbers of charred remains representing food plants were found in all the samples. These included a single charred free-threshing wheat (*Triticum aestivum/turgidum*) grain, wheat (*Triticum* ssp) and a few grains of barley (*Hordeum vulgare* L.), both are common cereal grains in the Medieval periods (Dyer 2006). Occasional flecks of charcoal were also seen in all samples. These remains are likely to have entered the sediments during flooding.

In general the plant macro-remains are very similar to those found by Monckton (2002) in a previous study of palaeochannels uncovered in the area nearby at the original Hemington Quarry.

The wide range of remains and habitats represented by the plant assemblage can be explained by the energy of the water during the flood which had probably disturbed the bottom of the river and also transported plants from the land areas affected by the flood. It is also possible that some of the plants are of earlier date and represent re-deposited material. However, the water plants and waterside plants suggest the vegetation near the channels which were surrounded by damp grassland probably used as pasture. Some food waste as charred cereals washed into the area from medieval occupation in the locality.

Conclusions

The analysis of wood and environmental samples from the Hemington Quarry extensions have provided evidence about the construction and use of the fish weirs and the possible environment of the area around the time the flood took place. It has also provided a new data for comparison with two other fish weirs recovered from the River Trent.